Selected and Current Works

BDP

Selected and Current Works

First published in Australia in 1998 by
The Images Publishing Group Pty Ltd
ACN 059 734 431
6 Bastow Place, Mulgrave, Victoria, 3170
Telephone (61 3) 9561 5544 Facsimile (61 3) 9561 4860
Email: books@images.com.au

National Library of Australia Cataloguing-in-Publication Data

Building Design Partnership
BDP: selected and current works.

Bibliography.
ISBN 1 86470 045 9

1. Building Design Partnership. 2. Architecture–Great Britain–
Designs and plans. 3. Architecture–Designs and plans. 4. Architec-
ture, Modern–20th century–Great Britain. 5. Architectural firms–
Great Britain. I. Title. II. Title: Building Design Partnership.
(Series: Monograph Series/(Images Publishing Group)).

724.6

BDP Editor: Jane Stephenson
BDP Photo Editor: Liz Earwaker
Edited by Stephen Dobney
Designed by The Graphic Image Studio Pty Ltd,
Mulgrave, Australia
Film by Scanagraphix Australia Pty Ltd
Printed in Hong Kong

Photography Credits

Aerofilms Ltd: 13 (4)
Allsport UK Ltd: 12 (2)
Roger Ball: 55 (4); title page
David Barbour: 28 (2, 3); 56 (1, 2); 60 (1, 2); 69 (3)
Andy Borzyskowski: 15 (6); 16 (1); 18 (1, 2); 44 (2), 56 (1, 2)
Alastair Carew Cox: 55 (3)
Reproduced from 1998 Ordnance Survey Map
with permission of the Controller of HMSO
© Crown Copyright AR35527R: 32 (1)
Peter Durant: 57 (3)
EDAW on behalf of Manchester Millennium Ltd: 32 (1)
Chris Edgecombe: 39
Jeff Faraday: 50 (6)
Dennis Gilbert: 64 (2, 3); 66 (2); 67; 68 (4, 5, 6); and end papers
Martine Hamilton-Knight: 24 (2); 25 (3); 26 (4, 5, 6); 27; 38 (1, 2); 69 (1)
Paul Highnam/CADW Welsh Historic Monuments: 20 (2, 3)
Christopher Hill: 35 (2, 3)
Keith Hunter: 70 (1, 2, 3, 4); 71 (1, 2, 3); 72 (2); 73 (3, 4); 74 (5, 6, 7); 75
Kitchenham Ltd: 48 (2)
Phil Mastores: 65 (1, 2); 69 (2)
Sally-Ann Norman: 54 (1, 2); 55 (5)
QA Photos Ltd: 41 (2); 42 (3, 4)
Paul Raftery: 61 (1)
Shepherd: 29 (4)
Rupert Truman: 20 (1); 21 (1, 2, 3); 22 (1, 2); 23 (3); 43 (6); 65 (3)
Tony Weller: 43 (5)
White House Studios: 72 (1)
Jonty Wilde: 23 (4)
Charlotte Wood: 12 (1, 3); 14; 48 (1); 49 (3); 50 (4); 62 (1, 2); 63 (3)

Contents

Introduction

BDP At The Leading Edge

By Dennis Sharp

The position of Building Design Partnership (also known as BDP) as one of the leading international practices in terms of fees earned—and as the largest firm of its kind in Europe—rests on its inter-disciplinary and multi-professional structure. Such a basis has allowed BDP to offer a wide variety of services.

Today, with an annual turnover of around £35 million (US$58.5 million), BDP is a highly efficient firm. In an age of aggrandisement, when size and magnitude often obscure good design and production, BDP has demonstrated the many advantages to be gained by professional teamwork and project management. The firm's current success is based on an original and historic partnership concept. When BDP was set up it was inspired by the idea of a multi-disciplinary professionalism, although few, if any, British architectural practices had any experience in working that way. Architecture was and still is BDP's central concern and with this focus it remains unique in Britain, offering a range of services far more comprehensive than other practices. Its built record is impressive. Moreover, it has recently gained design stature and is now often found competing for commissions on level ground with some of the leading European "signature" architects.

Now a limited company, BDP was originally established in 1961 out of the Grenfell-Baines architectural firm, which had operated since 1936. Since then it has pioneered the kind of consultancy practice that British construction industry advisers have hankered after for many years. Indeed it may be said that they have often overlooked an exemplary model on their own doorstep, and one that dates back nearly 40 years.

There is every reason to believe that BDP as a multi-disciplinary design organisation was inspired by the professional co-operation that existed during the years of World War II. The co-operative nature of those war years and the maturity of those returning to the professions after time in the services were responsible for bringing the REME (or Royal Engineers) mentality into "civvy street". It was Britain's wartime spirit, rather than the overt socialistic agendas of pre-war "co-operative" practices such as Tecton and ACP, that brought about the concept of multi-disciplinary practice.

These earlier firms had begun their teamwork from a perceived social agenda, and architects themselves had defined their professional needs. Their efforts provided the germ of this new concept of integration but they were hamstrung by RIBA regulations. However offices such as the London County Council (LCC) Architects Department, those of Hertfordshire, Essex and Nottingham counties, and eventually BDP, YRM, Arup Associates and RMJM in the private sector, reaped the harvest in the immediate post-war era. As restrictive practices eased, wider opportunities became available for co-operation across the disciplines. While taking advantage of these opportunities, BDP has remained focused on architectural practice as the central creative discipline.

Finding New Ways

The strength of BDP's design philosophy was characterised for me by one of the directors, who spoke of "finding new ways to deal with familiar circumstances". BDP's policy remains firmly based on a strongly held and convincing philosophy established in teamwork. This inter-disciplinary and multi-professional approach had its roots in the original partnership of the broad-minded George Grenfell-Baines. Professor Sir George Grenfell-Baines (now in his 91st year) is still respectfully known as "GG" by all BDP's staff, regardless of their position in the firm or whether they have ever actually met or even seen him. GG stimulated architectural practice in Britain with his ideas for teamwork and "diversity without uniformity".

The late Professor William Lethaby, in his biography of the architect Philip Webb, spoke about the need for the modern architect "to accept a rational theory of his art and develop its consequences in practice". This was to a very large degree what GG was on about. Rational processes were high on the agenda in a multi-disciplinary practice. They helped solve some of the tricky technological problems of the post-war world during a depressed but optimistic period.

In an article on Michael Scott's Dublin Bus Station in the *AA Journal* of June 1953, GG wrote about the "austerity ridden architects" of that time who "delight in natural association and harmony, a feeling reaching a climax in a [building] where structural necessity turns into a particularly happy and elegant expression". A few years later he would have had similar things to say about BDP's own masterpiece, the bus station at Preston, designed in a robust tribute to Paul Rudolph's parking garage at New Haven, Connecticut (1959–63). GG's own architectural predilections were broadly those of his British contemporaries. They included the inter-war town halls in Stockholm (by Asplund) and Hilversum (by Dudok) and London's 1951 Royal Festival Hall, as well as Scott's bus terminal—all buildings that involved a variety of professional disciplines and were enriched by artists and craftsmen.

What is often forgotten is that the various initiatives in professional architectural firms after the war—from the specialist offices to the multi-disciplinary ones—originated with the Modernist international movements of the inter-war period. At that time there was a belief in the principle that the role of the architect was to lead by design. To collaborate closely with other disciplines in order to produce a "total" solution to any problem was part and parcel of this approach, whether for the layout of a region, a town, or a housing estate, or the design of a factory or shop. BDP has cultivated these principles.

Today the aim is still to achieve, even at the much larger operative scales at which we all work, the highest standards in technology, planning and appearance and, through good design, to offer value and service to the client body.

From Small Beginnings

What began as a relatively small inter-professional partnership inspired by values associated with the north of England—values about co-operation, hard work and economy—has today become a hydra-headed company with offices in five British regions. There is also a growing network in Europe, with bureaux in Frankfurt and Dublin, and associated offices in France, Spain and Germany within BDP International SC.

BDP now carries a UK staff of 750 in London, Manchester, Glasgow, Belfast and Sheffield, and covers a range of specialisms including architecture; civil, structural and services engineering; town planning; cost consultancy; project management; landscape design; interior design; lighting; acoustics; and graphics. BDP is well equipped to service large schemes and any number of specialist projects at any one time. It has proved itself on the international stage by winning many competitions, as well as receiving numerous architecture and design awards. Furthermore, it is constantly building up the sort of expertise and experience that could hardly be accumulated by a mono-professional office. This does not mean, however, that each office is subsumed into a giant anonymous body of designers: far from it. Each office has a distinct personality. The BDP way of working has always encouraged a wide latitude in design approaches and effective teamwork.

The partnership's portfolio is impressive. It ranges from the single building to the subtle and sensitive integration of old and new buildings and environments. It includes infilling the historic fabric of part of Edinburgh near the celebrated Edinburgh Castle with the new Scottish Widows Headquarters; producing a new Science Centre in Glasgow; designing a new headquarters complex for Opel at Rüsselsheim in Germany; renovating London's largest public concert venue, the Royal Albert Hall in Kensington; masterplanning and redeveloping the All England Lawn Tennis Club in Wimbledon; and planning the reorganisation of the internationally significant area around the Tower of London.

BDP's Regional Autonomy

There is a distinct autonomy to BDP's regional offices. The general framework of company policy sensitively responds to local issues and conditions. This ethos was nurtured in the original practice in Preston, north Lancashire, before it was overtaken by the stronger "pulling power" of the Manchester office.

As it is in a "Euro capital", BDP's London office is a far better magnet for new work today than it was in the 1960s, when BDP was more evenly distributed throughout the UK. The firm has also become more internationally aware, and its directors are clear about what that means for the future in terms of jobs and competitive opportunities.

The composition of BDP's regional offices is the prerogative of local chairmen appointed by the chief executive. The Glasgow office, for example, is exclusively an architectural office, employing some 64 qualified architects. It makes use of the input of other professionals from both inside and outside the firm on a more traditional consultancy basis. It is the largest architectural office in Scotland and it serves the local region exclusively, with an increasing workload of prestigious building projects, at a time when Scotland itself is affirming its own national identity and future.

However, even with the wide opportunities of freedom of expression and action that exist within BDP, the question of

personal recognition within an integrated company has to be faced. It is still a difficult question, as I found for myself in many discussions with staff members. No one likes to hide behind the bushes of anonymity. And anonymity is certainly not the name of the game in architecture today. To a large extent, BDP resolves this problem through a process of internal peer review that gives recognition to the directors and job professionals involved; individuals are also acknowledged in technical journals and national papers where there is now greater freedom of attribution. Balanced against the need to recognise individual contributions is the need to maintain a sense of well-being and co-operative goodwill that is central to the image of BDP.

BDP as Teamwork

Teamwork, of course, is BDP's ideal. Its usefulness and effectiveness depend on many inter-related factors: that team members work together harmoniously; that they respect each other's potential and capabilities; and, above all, that they respect the collective aims and goals of their partners in relation to client needs. While some organisations seem to be constantly embroiled in conflict about the roles and personalities of their directors, BDP appears stable, consistent and content, allowing the firm to take on confidently some of the most ambitious and prestigious commissions in Europe.

Teamwork is as much an attitude of mind as a way of working. Some would say it is a philosophy. In that sense it has a good history. Among the master masons of the medieval guilds, teamwork was a way of life. And years later at the German Bauhaus, itself a name borrowed from the guild idea of the "Bauhutte", Walter Gropius and others redefined it as a legitimate way of working. After leaving the Bauhaus, Gropius developed this philosophy in books such as *The New Architecture and the Bauhaus* (written in England in 1936), in which he made a plea for rational thinking about building in terms of materials, tools and methods of working. Gropius wrote: "My idea of the architect is as a co-ordinator." Later, in the USA, he put forward his ideas for teamwork by individualists—forming The Architect's Collaborative (TAC) in 1945—and for close professional co-operation in integrated offices. Soon after that time, George Grenfell-Baines, who was greatly influenced by Gropius's idea, together with his various colleagues, saw an opportunity for an integrated practice in Britain; from this beginning, the idea for BDP gradually evolved.

Less appreciated, perhaps, is the way a multi-professional office can strengthen the integration of learning as well as technological development within the framework of a single company. The so-called "law of company logic" is shared in BDP to the extent that the acquired intelligence becomes a research tool in its own right. It is nurtured by a close relationship between those who have traditionally dealt with the scientific aspects of design—typically the structural and services engineers—and the architects, whose skills are concentrated on planning, spatial, social and aesthetic issues.

In discussions with BDP directors in Glasgow and London, I got the impression of a keen competitiveness and a genuine desire to work together. This is not just for the sake of teamwork balance, but is a cohesive way of working that suggests a thoroughly integrated organisation based on mutual respect and co-operation as well as hard-edged realities. Teamwork is about co-operation and the ability to work in a profession that for centuries was dominated by practices that were "one man thick", as the late Professor Lethaby once remarked.

Like all good professional families, BDP has evolved from an original concept largely inspired by one man's vision and shared by a closely knit group of colleagues who were committed to the same idea. Gropius spoke in 1936 of the generation of Modern architects who had, with their obsession for the machine and their interest in space, almost exhausted their creative energies. He wrote: "The next generation will accomplish that refinement of forms, which will lead to their generalisation." It was that fanning out, that diaspora of fundamental Modernist ideas that gave firms such as TAC and BDP their *raison d'être*, linking the general dissemination of modern architectural ideas to a co-operative way of working on much larger scale projects such as the work at Folkestone, Wimbledon, Rüsselsheim and Edinburgh. The schemes are all featured in this monograph and demonstrate very different approaches.

A Multi-faceted Commission

Such schemes as the Channel Tunnel UK Terminal, one of the UK's major building and engineering projects of the past decade, exemplify BDP's comprehensive approach and the advantages of integrated design. Here at Folkestone the commitment to inter-disciplinary professional practice came into its own and made sense. It provided immediate economy of information and communication, and met the needs of all those involved in the design of the terminal and its interiors. These included specialists dealing with overall planning issues, landscaping, earthworks and infrastructure requirements. Other specialists guided the project itself through a sea of political manoeuvres that could clearly have beaten a less centralised organisation. Thus BDP developed the Folkestone site like a small community—with its public pavilions and utilitarian sheds—in order to accommodate a number of various sized structures on a plan its architects describe as one of "related grids providing a hidden basis for co-ordinating roads, structures, landscape and signs". Co-ordination of planning was the key to designing a facility that would be used by two distinct groups of users at the same time: those who arrive on foot at the Passenger Terminal Building; and those in cars who are transferring to or from the trans-channel trains. Users have commented on the smoothness of the complex operations that occur daily on the site.

Renewing Wimbledon

In 1992 the All England Lawn Tennis and Croquet Club appointed BDP to prepare a long-term masterplan for its Wimbledon site. The goal was to ensure that the Wimbledon Championships maintained their position as the world's premier tennis tournament. The 1997 Championships saw the completion of the first stage of the plan, which included a new Number 1 Court seating 11,000 spectators; a state-of-the-art Broadcast Centre housing international television and radio facilities; restaurants and hospitality areas; and new courts 18 and 19. Additionally, landscaped picnic terraces and water features were introduced above extensive underground service accommodation.

Wimbledon involved the whole spectrum of BDP specialisms, from urban design and architecture through structural, services and acoustics engineering to the minutiae of landscape design and plant maintenance. The BDP team won the competition with a low-profile scheme set in grounds somewhat akin to the partitioned garden of a large English country house but set on a high-tech platform of new infrastructure and low-slung underground broadcasting units. The scheme, at ground level, is concerned with opening up public spaces and revealing a previously underrated urban porosity on the site. The design creates a plethora of private and semi-private spaces for those players, officials and specialists who create the world tennis atmosphere, and connects these effortlessly to the great public event for which the club is famous. Careful consideration has been given to system design and to the spaces that lie between the private and the public realm. A ladder pattern of paths enables the public to criss-cross the spaces between the buildings, and reach the higher ground where the newly landscaped slope provides a viewing area for the large TV screen.

New public spaces snake along the sides of the big show courts, providing easy access to the numerous food and drink outlets and ancillary services. These create a middle ground which, tucked under the stands and clear of the main routes, becomes as busy as a Saturday street market during the annual two-week Wimbledon Championships. Here a new relationship between public and private spaces occurs, both in historical and architectural terms, bringing about a sense of unity and purpose for the whole grounds.

Adam Opel Haus, Rüsselsheim, Germany

At the huge automobile manufacturing campus at Rüsselsheim near Frankfurt am Main, the new BDP-designed headquarters building for Opel was opened in 1998 by Chancellor Kohl. One of the main architectural issues of the site was to add a new focus to a disparate group of existing buildings, which also included one or two distinguished warehouse-type structures used for research and development. The new six-storey headquarters building for the German-based arm of General Motors houses administration, finance and marketing functions. A dramatic and coherent new structure situated on one side of a busy road reflects its presence in a new artificial lake. The headquarters building is part of a larger plan for the whole site, which will be connected to a Communications Centre—"Opel Live"—completing the key part of the masterplan.

BDP has achieved a very high design standard as well as a high quality finished building. These were key factors in the competition-winning scheme, which sought a non-monumental architecture that was sympathetic to the town. Ease of communication among the various offices—none of which are hierarchically organised—allows Opel to operate its own effective kind of teamwork, thus providing the company with a good commercial asset value as well as what appears to be positive user satisfaction.

Science and Insurance Buildings

The view of BDP's London office as international and catalytic, and Glasgow as more pragmatic, looser in its responses to architecture and with strong feelings of local autonomy, is borne out in two recent projects.

A proposed interactive Glasgow Science Centre, hailed as "Scotland's most ambitious Millennium project", will soon be located on Pacific Quay, a prominent waterfront site on the south bank of the River Clyde. It is one of two major projects that have occupied the Glasgow office recently, alongside the continuing work on the £230 million (US$385 million) Braehead shopping centre, the Citizens' Theatre and the Nobel explosives museum. The Science Centre is to be situated on the edge of the River Clyde opposite Norman Foster's Armadillo Conference Centre, which it nicely complements. With commissions such as these, the computer-aided design and rendering skills that are common in all the federal parts of BDP provide compelling simulated images of the finished projects. They provide clients with visual data and analytical tools that allow them to see not only what they are getting from a design and layout point of view, but also the franchise, rental and developed spaces available in the building, thus enabling a fuller economic assessment to be made.

The other significant Scottish scheme is the new headquarters for insurance company Scottish Widows set on a formerly useless site in inner Edinburgh. The surrounding area has been smartened up recently by the addition of Terry Farrell and Partners' drum-shaped conference centre. Scottish Widows is a large development, which links its disparate elements around a fan-shaped atrium. The office elements are scaled down, offering opportunities to weld the bulky buildings into a finely balanced and sensitive urban intervention through a series of public walkthroughs and differing facades. Accomplishing this has needed considerable skill, as on one side of the site are terraced houses and on the exposed public side is the awesome bulk of Edinburgh's world famous castle.

Conclusion

BDP's continuing ability to attract the best professionals and graduates, and the readiness of those professionals to remain part of the practice—sometimes for their whole careers—are impressive indicators. Questioning some of these people about what it was that most attracted them to the practice, I invariably received the reply that it was related to being able to produce good architecture within a team, working closely with other professionals and seeing things built. *Sui generis*, this has been the setting and the lasting success of BDP for nearly four decades.

Dennis Sharp is a British architect, writer and critic. He was the founding editor of *AA Quarterly* and *World Architecture* and is the author of various books on 20th century architecture.

Leisure and Learning

Design for cultural and educational
activities is a major facet of BDP's
work and involves many locations of
national importance. There has been
a need to combine skills in specialist
functional design with those in historic
building restoration. Many institutions
have required long-term planning
before any buildings were designed,
and construction has then occurred
in several phases. Fruitful long-term
relationships are the basis of
success.

In all these examples we bring people
together in large numbers to be
entertained or informed. The theatrical
element is always present, showing
people to each other as they
congregate and work on many levels.
Respect for context and heritage,
however, produces a quite distinct
character in each project.

1

1   All England Lawn Tennis and Croquet Club long-term development plan: view from the east

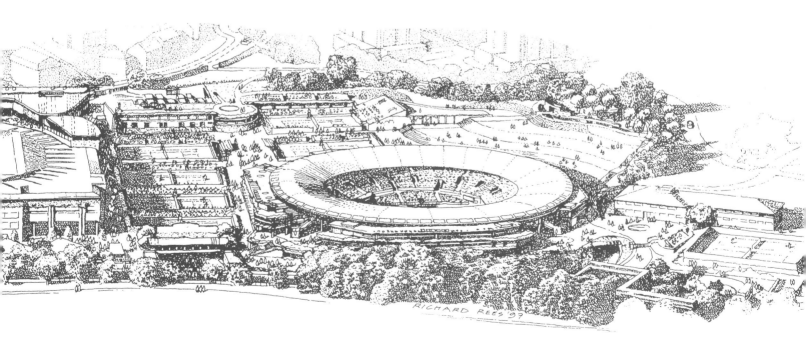

All England Lawn Tennis and Croquet Club
Masterplan, Stages 1 and 2A

Design/Completion 1992/2000
Wimbledon, London, England
All England Lawn Tennis and Croquet Club
30,000 square metres
Concrete frame with steel roof
Natural timber, rendered blockwork, glazing

The key objectives of the masterplan commissioned by the All England Club were to protect the long-term future of the tournament and to improve the quality of the event for all. The Club's brief was to create a relaxed and quintessentially Wimbledon atmosphere summed up as "tennis in an English garden".

Stage 1 of this plan was the new, 11,000-seat Number 1 Court. It has a steel cantilevered roof, a 12-sided seating bowl and accommodation terraces. Restaurants and hospitality suites are separated from the underside of the stadium's seating bowl to provide daylit access concourses which circle the bowl on two levels. Four corner entrances give access to these concourses.

The stadium is countersunk into the west-to-east facing hillside, and conceals a complex subterranean "back-of-house" area buried deep into the existing slope. The Broadcast Centre, a new three-storey brick building containing state-of-the-art facilities for television transmission, is also set deep into the hillside.

The landscape design has created a garden with background buildings, focusing attention on the trees, lawns, flowers and water features. The terraced hillside provides not only a sweeping backdrop to the new stadium, but a picnic area that enhances the English garden setting.

Stage 2A is a new facilities building (see figure 6) which will provide accommodation for players, members, press, umpires and officials. Three open elevations and the plan form and section of the building offer private and informal spaces, while still providing enjoyment of the activities of the Championships through spectacular views across various parts of the grounds.

1

2

3

4

1   New Number 1 Court: south-west corner
2   Stadium bowl
3   Hilltop landscape
4   Stage 1 with new Number 1 Court and Centre Court (foreground)

Opposite:
Hospitality terraces overlooking play
6   Model of Stage 2A facilities building west of
    Centre Court extension

6

National Tennis Centre

Design/Completion 1997/2002
Krylatskoye, Moscow, Russia
Bovis International (for the Russian National
Tennis Federation)
7,500 seats
Steel frame and tubular steel roof
Sheet steel cladding, timber

In 1996 BDP was commissioned by the
Organisational Committee of the National
Sports Centre in Moscow to prepare a
viability study for the National Tennis
Centre. The site is adjacent to the former
Olympic rowing competition site and
velodrome, on the western edge of
Moscow close to the river. The tennis
element in the southern half of the site is
focused around a multi-use arena court
with an opening roof for summer events
and tournaments.

7

Sydney Tennis Centre

Design/Completion 1998/1999
Homebush Bay, Sydney, Australia
Olympic Co-ordination Authority
10,000 seats
Main stadium: precast concrete with steel roof
Facilities building: steel structure with timber
facing and steel roof
Concrete, steel, timber facing

BDP has had a lead role in the design of
the new tennis centre on the Olympic site
at Homebush Bay, Sydney, as part of a
team led by Lawrence Nield and Partners,
Australia. The circular seating
arrangement of BDP's design for the
Wimbledon stadium was the generator for
the Sydney Centre Court. The stadium is
arranged in a symmetrical 24-sided seating
bowl. A shade roof covering 70 per cent of
the spectators is provided, as at the
Wimbledon stadium.

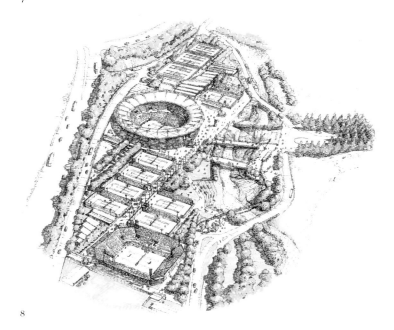

8

7   Model of the National Tennis Centre, Moscow,
    showing covered courts and stadium
8   Tennis Centre, Sydney

Royal Albert Hall

Design/Completion 1992/2003
Kensington Gore, London, England
The Corporation of the Hall of Arts and Sciences
33,800 square metres
Load-bearing brickwork and wrought iron
Brick, terracotta

BDP was commissioned to develop a concept design/masterplan for the first comprehensive refurbishment of the Royal Albert Hall since its construction in 1871. The project was informed by the need to respect the Grade I listed building and its structure.

The refurbishment is planned to improve conditions for the audience, both within the auditorium itself and throughout the foyers; to upgrade backstage accommodation for artists and staff; to enable the management to put on a wider variety of shows and other events; and to enhance the setting of the building and the public spaces around it. The work is phased over a number of years to avoid disrupting the programme of events.

In addition to the extensive works within the existing building, an underground service yard will be excavated below the terraces and gardens of the south steps of the Hall. This will give direct access to the stage and to new catering facilities, dressing rooms and plant rooms in the basement. The roadway around the Hall will then be paved over to create a major new public pedestrian space. A new south porch will be added, which will enable public circulation throughout the Hall to be improved.

1

1   Model of new south porch
2   Section through new south steps development and remodelled Hall

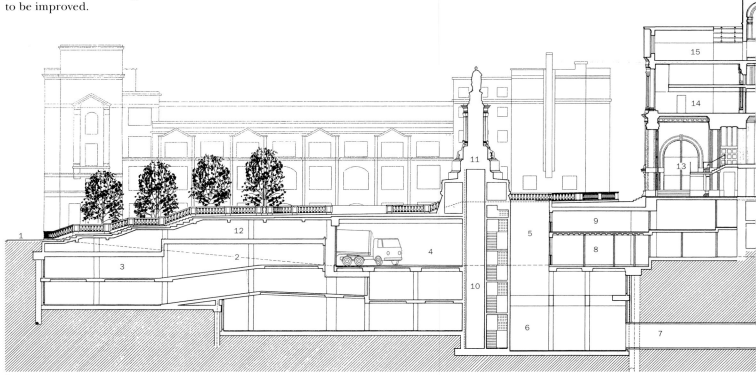

2

16

KEY
1 Prince Consort Road
2 Access ramp to service yard
3 Residents' car park
4 Service yard
5 Air intake shaft
6 Ventilation plant room
7 Ventilation tunnel
8 Workshops and store
9 Dressing rooms and show management
10 Fire-fighting lift and stairs
11 Memorial to the exhibition of 1851
12 Heat rejection plant
13 New south porch
14 Administrative offices
15 Refreshment room
16 Restored gallery
17 Restored organ
18 Restaurant
19 Ticket shop
20 Stage
21 New storage and assembly area with lift access to stage and arena
22 Level access between service yard and assembly area
23 Restored ornamental plaster work of cove
24 New acoustic velarium to replace the "mushrooms"
25 Rebuilt circle tier
26 New arena foyers
27 Auditorium ventilation distributed through plenums below the seats
28 North porch
29 Kensington Gore

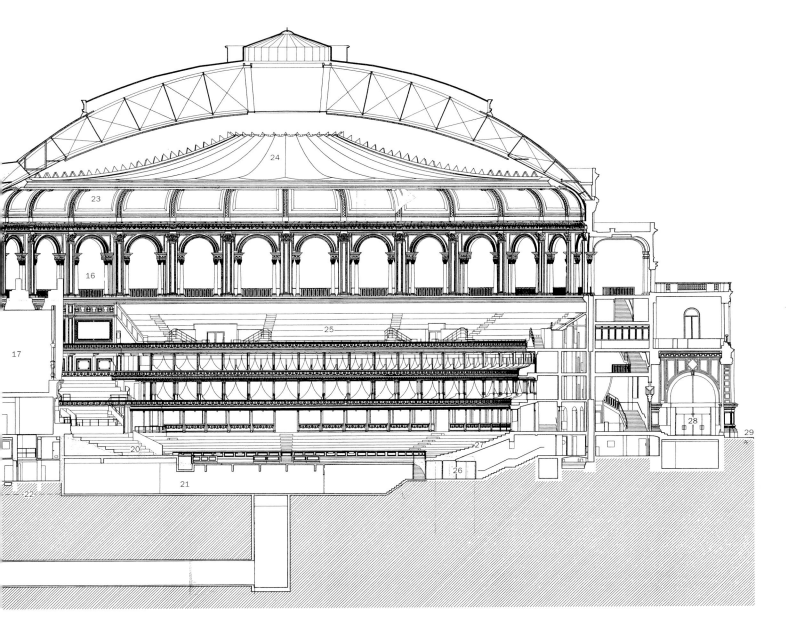

Neptune Court, National Maritime Museum

Design/Completion 1992/1998
Greenwich, London, England
Trustees of the National Maritime Museum
8,000 square metres
Steel-ribbed shell supported by load-bearing masonry
Hollow section steel roof; new floor; reinforced concrete structure

The National Maritime Museum, one of the world's finest maritime museums, is housed in a group of Grade I listed buildings in the Royal Park of Greenwich, adjacent to the Royal Naval College. Mindful of the historic importance of the listed buildings, a masterplan was drawn up to enhance visitor experience, increase visitor numbers, improve operations and rationalise the museum's estate. BDP has also completed interior remodelling of the original space.

The radical reconfiguration of the galleries is centred on a new arrival space and introductory gallery under a new glazed roof within the existing courtyard. BDP, with Rick Mather Architects, designed the Neptune Court to increase gallery space by one-third and to improve greatly orientation and circulation.
The roof, supported only on the parapets of the existing masonry, takes the form of a glass "pillow" supported by a grid of minimal trusses.

1

1 Roof over Neptune Court
2 Model
3 Perspective of Neptune Court

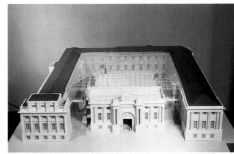
2

3

Plas Mawr

Design/Completion 1993/1997
Conwy, North Wales
Cadw: Welsh Historic Monuments
1,350 square metres
External masonry walls, internal timber frame
Rendered rubble, oak, slate

Constructed between 1576 and 1585, Plas Mawr (the Great House) is regarded as the finest surviving Elizabethan town house in Britain. In 1993 the house was placed in the care of Cadw: Welsh Historic Monuments. BDP was appointed as architect and design team leader to undertake an extensive programme of research, investigation, recording and repair to secure the long-term conservation of the building.

Plas Mawr had survived almost unaltered, and is especially rich in its original carpentry, fitted woodwork and decorative plasterwork. Maximum retention of the original fabric was a key objective. However, long-term decay and inadequate resources had led to extensive structural and fabric failure, some areas being on the point of local collapse. The conservation strategy sought to use the materials and techniques available to the original builders, to undo previous inappropriate repairs, and to ensure the reinstatement of original load paths, component functions and spatial functions.

1

2

1 Rendered gabled exterior
2 Decorative plasterwork in great chamber
3 Restored roof beams

3

1830 Warehouse

Design/Completion 1988/1997
Castlefield, Manchester, England
Trustees of the Museum of Science and Industry,
Manchester
10,000 square metres
Load-bearing walls, timber-framed bays
Brickwork, timber, slate

The project entailed the conservation of the world's oldest standing railway building, a four-storey warehouse built in 1830, which stood at one end of the world's first public railway line, the Liverpool to Manchester Railway. Before any restoration was started, detailed archaeological, photographic and dimensional surveys were carried out, involving the identification and recording of every component.

The repair of the building and its conversion to museum use was carried out in three phases to respond to available funding. The conservation approach was led by the desire to retain as much as possible of the original fabric as standing industrial archaeology and to keep modern interventions to a minimum. Building repairs were undertaken in a simple, comprehensible manner and discreetly date-stamped. New circulation and service facilities were designed in a clearly articulated contemporary style to contrast with the original structure. Visitors can therefore "read" both the original building and the recent conservation works.

1

2

3

1   Multiple bays of carriage shed
2   Lift enclosure
3   Former carriage access

Eureka! The Children's Museum

Design/Completion 1990/1992
Halifax, Yorkshire, England
Trustees of Eureka!
4,500 square metres
Steel frame, in situ and precast concrete floors
Sandstone masonry, glass, sheet metal roofing

The aim of this learning centre for children of primary school age is to educate them about the world they live in through hands-on participation and interactive exhibitions. Built on a 5-hectare site close to the centre of Halifax, it attracts some 400,000 visitors a year. As a new building, it was designed to be contemporary in form and detail, and to respect its conservation area neighbours in massing and material while creating an environment that is appealing and stimulating to younger children.

Three elevations are of masonry, while the fourth is curved and completely glazed, revealing the exhibits inside. A triangular stone wall breaks through this glazed elevation at an oblique angle, defining the building entrance. From within, the glazed wall affords spectacular views and acts as the principal point of orientation. The building is itself an exhibit, revealing its construction and inner functions, and how these respond when the building is in use.

The accommodation is basically an open plan two-storey exposition hall with a services distribution grid to allow maximum flexibility for change and development. The project was the first of its type in the UK and has become an exemplar.

1

1   Eureka! Museum (foreground) and Halifax plc
    Headquarters (background; see also page 69)
2   Museum approach
3   Glazed entrance elevation
4   Archimedes in his bath

2

3

4

St Peter's Campus, University of Sunderland, Phases I & II

Design/Completion 1990/1996
Monkwearmouth, Sunderland, England
University of Sunderland
20,742 square metres
In situ concrete structural frame
Exposed concrete, cedar, aluminium, brick

On a 10-hectare, south-sloping site on the north bank of the River Wear, the University of Sunderland in north-east England is creating a second major campus for 8,000 students. BDP prepared the masterplan for St Peter's Campus and has designed and built two of the proposed four phases.

The campus plan creates a strong communal identity, closely related to the urban fabric of the riverside and city. Building forms and urban spaces promote energy-conscious solutions in the use of available daylight and solar warmth, and protection from inclement weather. An integrated urban environment has been successfully achieved by mixing educational activities and public amenities.

Phase I comprises the Business School and the Learning Amenity Buildings, loosely structured along the south ecclesiastical axis that connects the adjacent seventh century St Peter's Church and Holy Trinity Church on the south side of the Wear.

Continued

1   Roof plan of Phases I and II
2   View across the River Wear
3   Phase I buildings

1

2

3

Buildings have been set into the slope and links provided between upper and lower levels. A clear sectional strategy down the site allows buildings to be entered at the top and bottom of the slope, with pedestrian routes within the campus running along the contour lines.

Phase II comprises a new School of Computing and Information Services, which encloses the east side of the street leading from St Peter's Church into the university's spatial heart. It also forms a protective backdrop to University Square, a sloping piazza that provides a sheltered southerly aspect and views of the river.

The computer school has as its heart a space housing more than 500 computer workstations for open access use. To accommodate this large space sensitively on the sloping site, the computer hall is designed on three open terraces, stepping down the site at 1.2-metre-high intervals, linked by a ramped internal street. Looking down the sloping street a very animated interior has been created—both an interactive and a social space.

The design for the second stage of the Learning Resource Centre creates a new "finger" linking it into the first phase. From this emerged the idea of the reading room within the courtyard: a sanctuary for quiet study away from the keyboard noise. With the double ground level approach, a deck has been created at upper ground level for students to read in the open air, protected by the wrap of the building.

A consistent palette of materials was chosen to create harmony among the buildings while respecting their individual character, and to withstand the harsh marine environment.

4

5

6

Hampden Gurney Primary School

Design/Completion 1997/2000
Marylebone, London, England
John Laing Developments
1,800 square metres (teaching and non-teaching areas);
1,600 square metres (play areas)
Steel frame with in situ concrete floor slabs
Brickwork walls, glass balustrades, hardwood floors and window frames,
PTFE fabric roof canopy

To replace the 1960s Hampden Gurney Church of England Primary School in Marylebone with a new school and nursery on the same site, a residential development of 52 apartments was proposed, the sale of which would fund the new 240-pupil school. The apartments are in two L-shaped blocks framing an interior garden, with the school at one corner.

The new school is planned on six levels, with the ground floor raised to create a covered play area in the undercroft. The traditional playground has been divided into smaller play "territories" for different age groups of children. Each of the five storeys of teaching space has its own corresponding play garden, which is reached by bridges across the central six-storey lightwell. Each play garden is contained within the building, and is therefore covered by the floor above, but is also open to natural light and air. A rooftop technology garden provides a nature workshop and weather station.

1

2

3

1 Central six-level atrium
2 Play gardens face the street
3 New school between apartment buildings
4 Atrium, Sheffield Hallam University
5 Perspective, Tipperary RBDI

The Atrium Building, Sheffield Hallam University

Design/Completion 1991/1994
Sheffield, Yorkshire, England
Sheffield Hallam University, Cormorant plc
24,500 square metres
Steel frame
Curtain wall, brickwork cladding, glazed atrium roof

Sheffield Hallam is one of the largest universities in the UK with more than 20,000 students. A masterplan was prepared by Bond Bryan Partnership to concentrate the scattered facilities onto the steeply sloping city centre campus. To link the existing buildings, 21,500 square metres of new accommodation and circulation were inserted in the first phase. The key element was a central atrium, a much needed focus and heart to the campus, for which BDP won the commission.

The atrium is overlooked on four glazed levels by the new and existing teaching blocks. The design form is multi-layered, stepping back to provide areas of seating for informal study, meeting and simple enjoyment of the space.

4

Tipperary Rural and Business Development Institute

Design/Completion 1997/1999
Thurles, County Tipperary, Ireland
Tipperary Rural and Business Development Institute
Phase I: 4,685 square metres
In situ reinforced concrete with exposed coffered ceilings
Fair-face blockwork and render

This third-level training institute is for 1,000 full-time students. The accommodation provides a mix of traditional classrooms and engineering science laboratories, a library and virtual library, computer laboratories and lecture theatres. From the focal point of the entrance block and reception, other blocks radiate via a pedestrian street. A feature of the exterior is the circular pond surrounding the entrance block.

5

Regeneration and Movement

The making and mending of city fabric is an unending task. BDP's strong interest in urban design has led to a variety of projects involving the regeneration of public places, city districts and commercial centres. How people arrive and move through urban space is crucial to the quality and liveliness of that space.

BDP has worked on major transport projects embedded in cities and also on free-standing facilities of unprecedented technology and scale. The practice has a long record of designing for unique situations and of steering urban projects through the political process.

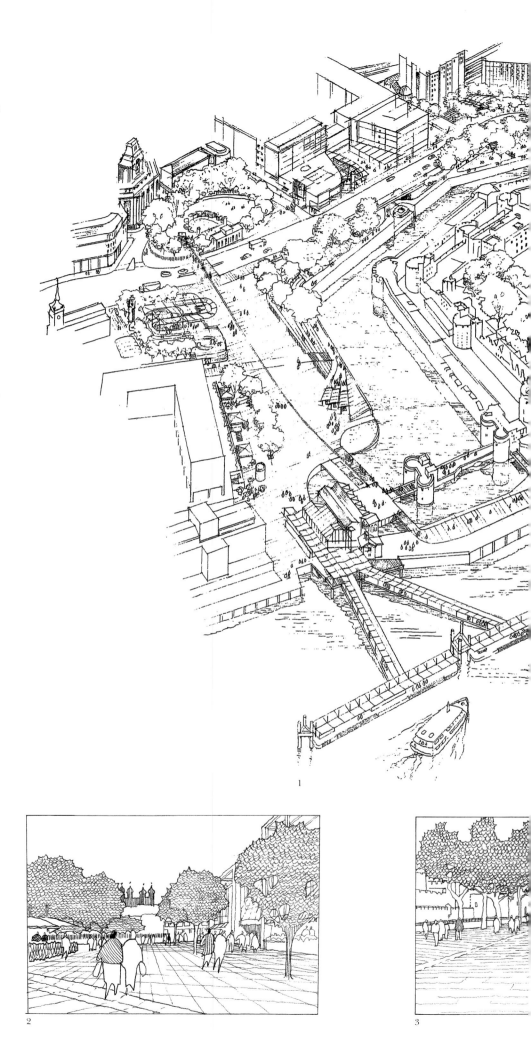

1

2

3

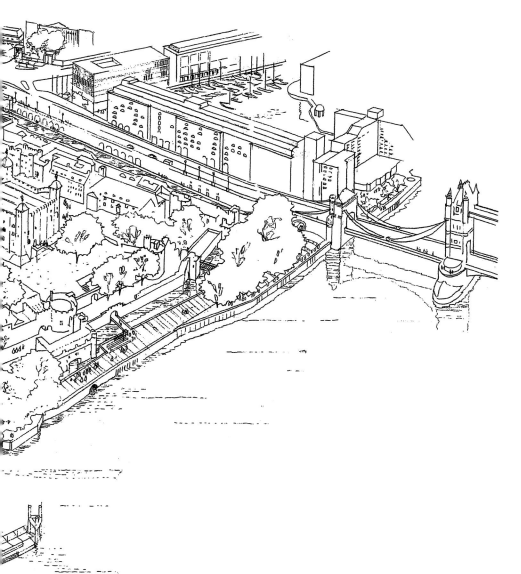

The Tower of London Environs

Design/Completion 1997/ongoing
Tower Hill, London, England
Historic Royal Palaces Agency, Port of London
Authority, London Borough of Tower Hamlets,
Taylor Woodrow Property Company
30 hectares

A masterplan to transform the immediate surroundings of the Tower of London has been prepared by BDP as lead consultant. The improvements to this World Heritage site are part of a wider plan to enhance the Pool of London—the stretch of the River Thames between and surrounding London Bridge and Tower Bridge.

The Tower of London is a major international visitor destination that suffers from a degraded environment, pedestrian and vehicular conflict, poor visitor and transportation facilities, and a confusing array of signs and street furniture.

Projects to address these problems include redeveloping the underground station with a new station and mixed-use building; realigning one of London's most significant east–west trunk roads; creating a new civic space; relandscaping public spaces and gardens; improving pedestrian movement at the gateways to the Tower, including subways; replacing Tower Pier; and reflooding the moat.

The project also included an urban design analysis of future development opportunities in the areas surrounding the Tower, given its juxtaposition to the City of London.

1   Masterplan
2   New public square to north-east
3   Pedestrian access created along the riverside wharf
4   New moat walkway to the east

4

Central Manchester Regeneration

Design/Completion 1996/1999 (Marks &
Spencer store)
Manchester, England
Manchester Millennium Ltd, Marks & Spencer
plc, Prudential Assurance
25,000 square metres (retail)

As part of the masterplan to rebuild
central Manchester following the
devastating bomb explosion in June 1996,
BDP is working on three major
commissions.

The first project is to replan the area
around Manchester Cathedral, Chethams
School of Music and the frontage of the
River Irwell. To establish a new setting for
these historic buildings in a riverside park,
the closure of two streets and the removal
of a redundant river bridge is proposed.
This park, adjacent to the main shopping
district, will re-establish the cathedral as a
major focal point in the city.

At the heart of the masterplan lies the site
of the Marks & Spencer store which was
destroyed by the bomb. The new store will
be the largest Marks & Spencer store in
the world. It extends beyond the site of
the former store and focuses on a galleria
connecting Corporation Street and New
Cathedral Street.

The third area of the city's rebuilding
scheme is Shambles West, a mixed-use
development which re-establishes a city
block and a network of pedestrian streets
forming the west side of New Cathedral
Street. The scheme provides street level
and first floor retailing, with apartments
above facing onto Deansgate.

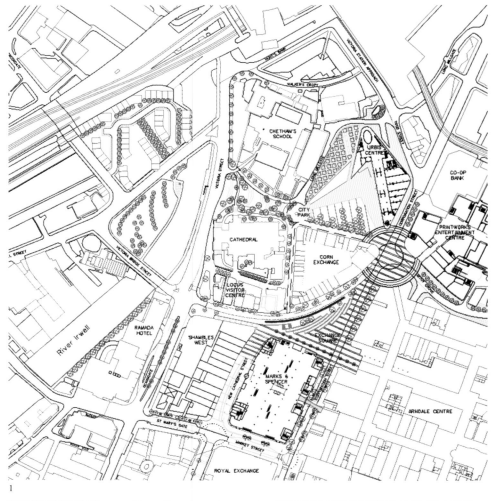

1

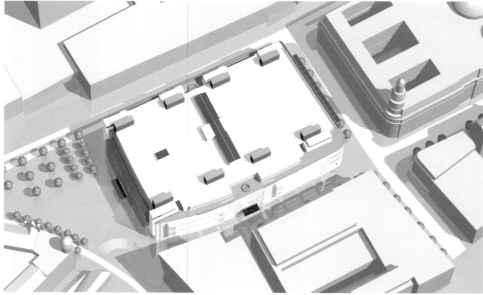

2

3

4

1   Masterplan including riverside park,
    Marks & Spencer store and Shambles West
2   Model of Marks & Spencer store
3   South-west frontage: view along New
    Cathedral Street towards Exchange Square
4   View towards north facade across Exchange Square

Bracknell Town Centre Redevelopment

Design/Completion 1997/2005
Bracknell, Berkshire, England
Allied London Properties plc, Schroder Exempt
Property Unit Trust
39 hectares

Bracknell was developed in the 1950s and
1960s as a second generation New Town,
strategically located to the west of London.
In recent years the town centre has
become run down and in need of
redevelopment. The town's retail area
requires substantial enhancement,
together with the introduction of a variety
of new and complementary leisure,
cultural, residential, civic and commercial
office uses.

The masterplan covers the area bounded
by the town centre ring road. It
substantially reconfigures this area to
provide a more integrated and interesting
juxtaposition of facilities and space.

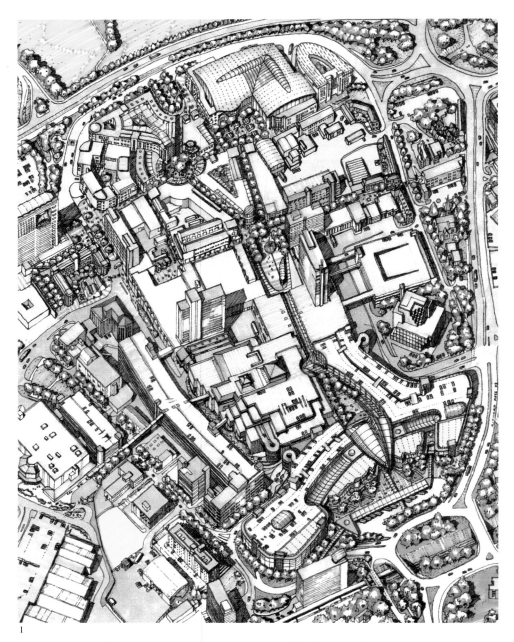

1

Duke Street/Bold Street Urban Regeneration

Design/Completion 1998/2001
Liverpool, England
Duke Street Partnership
37 hectares

The first integrated physical, social and
economic action plan in the country has
been approved for the Duke Street/Bold
Street quarter of central Liverpool, an
undeveloped area of enormous potential.

The Duke Street/Bold Street area will be
the focus of a three-pronged, fully
integrated approach to regeneration:
investment in a complete overhaul of the
public realm with around 40 separate
building projects; investment in training
and employment initiatives; and an
extensive business support programme
geared towards the local residential
community.

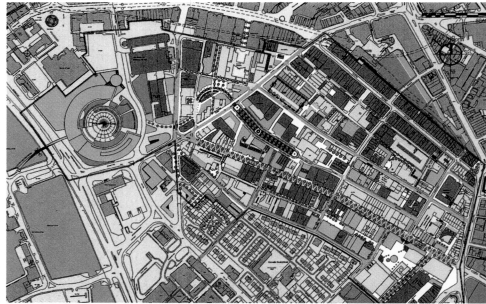

2

1   Axonometric of Bracknell
2   Masterplan of Duke Street/Bold Street

34

Laganside Regeneration

Design/Completion 1987/1996 (ongoing)
Belfast, Northern Ireland
Belfast Harbour Commissioners, Laganside
Development Corporation, Ulsterbus, Northern
Ireland Transport Holding Company

In 1987 the Department of the Environment for Northern Ireland commissioned BDP (with Shepheard Epstein and Hunter) to prepare a masterplan for a 4-kilometre stretch of the River Lagan, which flows through the centre of Belfast to the docks. This masterplan identified a number of areas which had development opportunities.

BDP subsequently prepared a masterplan for one of these areas, Clarendon Dock, and designed the infrastructure that has laid the foundations for a dramatic change to this 12-hectare site. The plan for Laganside is being implemented by a development corporation.

The transport hub of the regenerated area is the new bus centre designed by BDP. One of the primary design considerations was to combine the bus station and the 300-space car park above into a single architectural unit. Topping the building is a canopy which completes the composition of the main elevation and gives the building a presence on the Belfast skyline.

Pedestrians enter through a double-height steel and glass foyer; the concourse elevation is glazed to maximise daylight. Within the concourse, the division between public and private space is marked by a wall of toughened glass which opens for ticket counters and other points of contact.

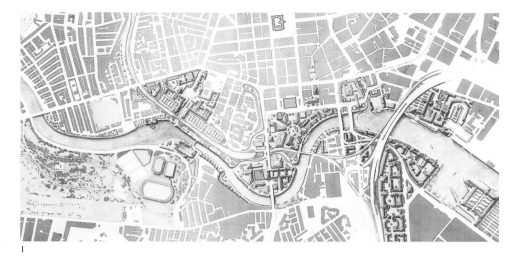

1

2

3

1   Concept plan identifying development
    opportunities on Laganside
2   Bus centre on the waterfront
3   Interior of bus centre

Glasgow Science Centre

Design/Completion 1994/2001
Pacific Quay, Glasgow, Scotland
Glasgow Development Agency
11,700 square metres (Exploratorium);
2,150 square metres (Imax cinema)
In situ reinforced concrete frame, steel outer shell
Glass, granite, titanium

The £71 million Glasgow Science Centre is the centrepiece of the Glasgow Development Agency's Pacific Quay masterplan, which has won Millennium funding. In common with the best examples world-wide, the Science Centre aims to bridge the gap between scientific knowledge, current technology, and future trends and developments. The Science Centre will help foster a greater understanding of and regard for science by using everyday examples of applied science to which visitors can easily relate in a "hands on", interactive way.

Continued

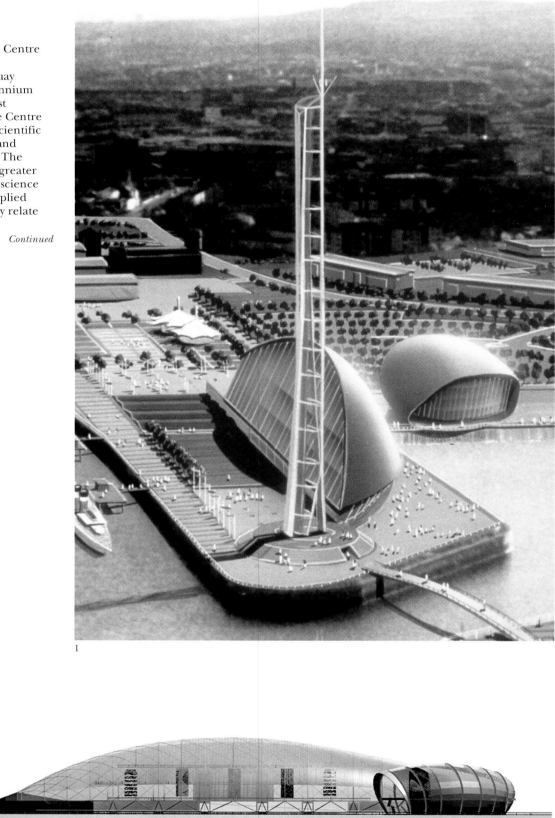

1

2

3

The design strategy is to create a building which is both an icon and a container expressing the spirit and function of the interactive exhibits it contains. A south-facing, curved, reflective titanium-clad wing protects the building from the elements; in contrast, the sheer glass north-facing wall allows maximum light to enter the building and provides extensive views over the River Clyde and the city beyond.

A 350-seat 2D/3D large-format Imax cinema sits adjacent to the Exploratorium, and a 100-metre-high Millennium Tower (by Richard Horden) is connected to the Exploratorium via an underground pedestrian link.

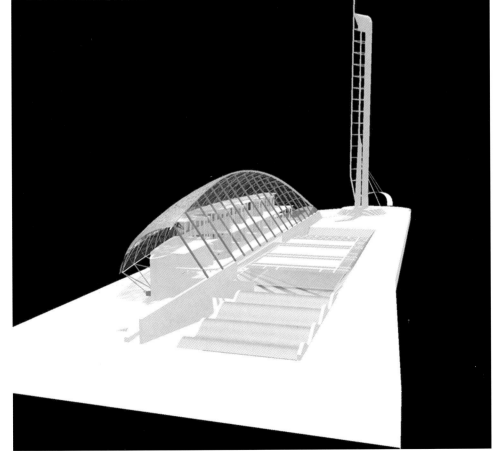

1   Glasgow Science Centre at Pacific Quay
2   Millennium Tower, Exploratorium and Imax cinema from the south
3   Titanium-clad south edge of Exploratorium
4   View from north-east

4

Vasco da Gama Centre

Design/Completion 1996/1998–2000
Lisbon, Portugal
Sonae Imobiliaria
60,000 square metres
Concrete
Aluminium and glass cladding, steel and glass
roof

Following an international competition, BDP was appointed by leading Portuguese developer Sonae to design the Vasco da Gama Centre. It is the major commercial development for Expo Urbe, the Lisbon regeneration project with Expo 98 at its heart.

Expo 98 took place on a large disused docklands site to the east of the city. The intention was not only to stage a major world event, but also to regenerate this area with many permanent buildings, as part of Lisbon's long-term development strategy.

The Vasco da Gama Centre is linked to Oriente Station, a major new transport interchange designed by Santiago Calatrava. During Expo 98 the central mall acted as the gateway to the fair. The mall spine has a dramatic 35 metre by 140 metre glazed roof bordered above by landscaped terraces.

The retail, leisure and restaurant elements occupy four levels of the sloping site. The commercial area of the centre will later be flanked by two 24-storey towers, providing a total of 40,000 square metres of residential space.

1

1   View of Oriente Station from the mall
2   Looking towards the centre from the station
3   Model of the completed Vasco da Gama project

2

UK Channel Tunnel Terminal

Design/Completion 1989/1994
Folkestone, Kent, England
Transmanche Link
142 hectares
Passenger terminal building: concrete frame, metal mast, stainless steel cables
White aluminium cladding panels, planar and aluminium glazing, PTFE-coated glasscloth roof

The brief to design the UK Channel Tunnel Terminal was wide-ranging, encompassing the overall co-ordination of the site layout, and the planning and design of the infrastructure, buildings, landscape, interiors and signage.

The terminal is sandwiched into a long, narrow site of high landscape value between the North Downs and the M20 motorway. The masterplan organises the elements so that vehicles en route to France move diagonally across the site from the south-west corner through tolls, frontier controls and queuing lanes, and approach the train carriers from the foot of the scarp slope.

The brief for the 18 buildings on the site called for modern, coherent, co-ordinated references to which both travellers and staff would respond positively. The

buildings are designed as elegant white pavilions in a green landscape—punctuation points along the traveller's route prior to the journey through the tunnel. The design strategy defined the public buildings as being open and transparent, while the operational activities take place within more closed and cellular forms.

The focal public building is the passenger terminal building, with its distinctive fabric roof, angled to the sun to allow changing light patterns to illuminate the central atrium. The roof becomes a beacon at night, presenting a strong reference point for the traveller.

The control centre performs the same role as the control tower of an airport. It has a simple geometric form and acts as a distinctive visual marker at the highest point on the site.

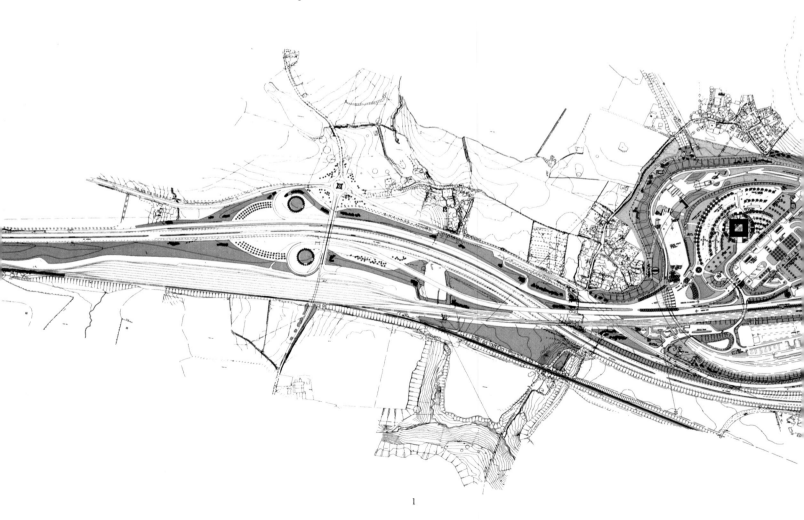

1

2

1   Site plan
2   Aerial view from the west

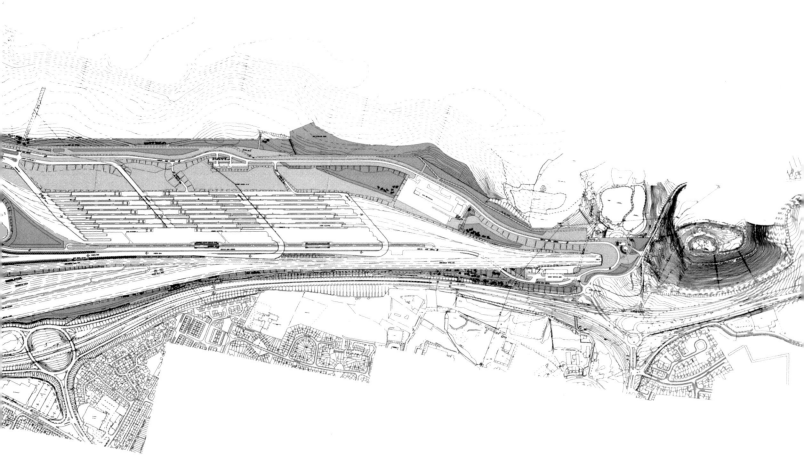

3

4

5

3 Aerial view of entire site with passenger terminal
   building (centre) and control centre (left)
4 Illuminated fabric roof
5 Detail of passenger terminal building
6 Glazed aperture in tensile roof

6

CrossRail

Design/Completion 1992–1995/post-2000
Central London, England
CrossRail Project Team
4 kilometres
NATM spray concrete lining
Precast polychromatic brick cladding to concourse,
copper lining to domed spaces

CrossRail will link the counties east and west of London to the centre with a new underground railway beneath the West End and the City. BDP has designed the four new deep stations at Bond Street, Tottenham Court Road, Farringdon and Liverpool Street in collaboration with the veteran Anglo-Swedish architect Ralph Erskine.

The concept for these stations is to create generously shaped spaces designed around the needs of the traveller. Passengers can wait in concourses alongside the 300-metre-long train. Gables set at carriage intervals carry information screens and services. Each concourse may be screened to create an environment free from the dust, heat and noise generated by the train and to reduce the danger of the platform edge.

Circulation between ticket halls and platform rooms will be via large vaulted spaces lined in textural brick and copper. Passengers will circulate vertically by means of escalators or lifts, with access available to everyone. This will create a more comfortable, secure and social environment, thereby encouraging a greater use of public transport through and within the capital.

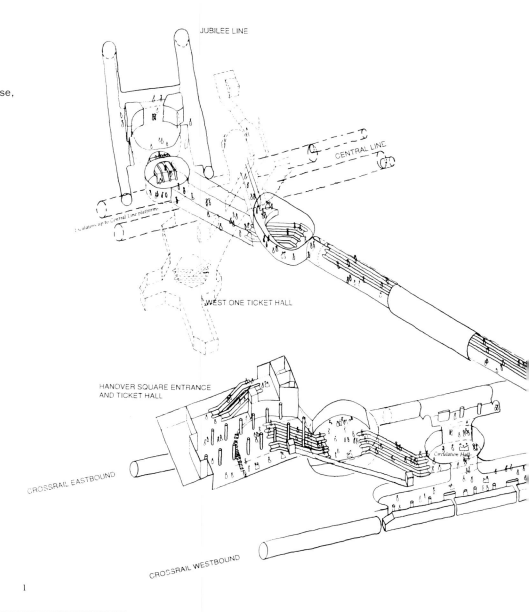

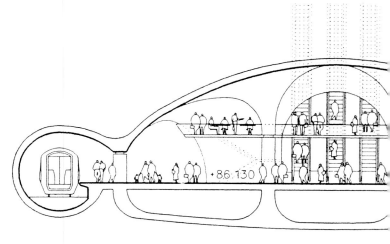

1 Original concept of Bond Street Station
2 Platform model
3 Section of Farringdon Station
4 Original concept of Bond Street Station below Hanover Square

44

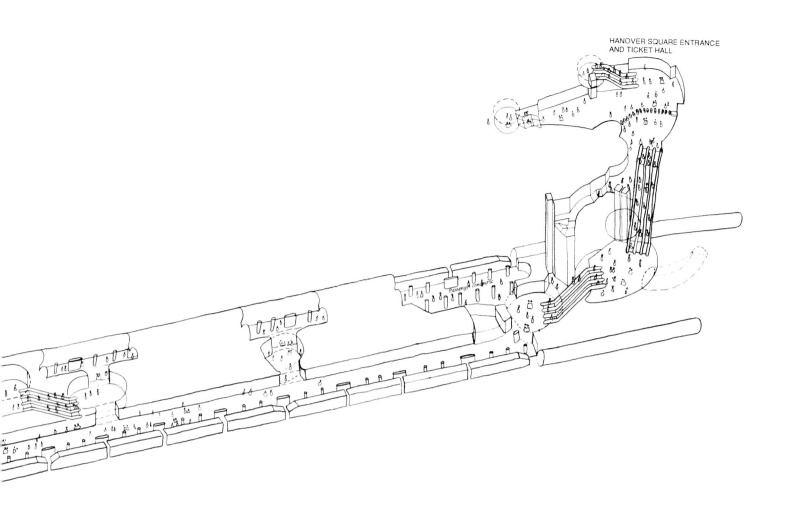

HANOVER SQUARE ENTRANCE
AND TICKET HALL

Passenger concourse

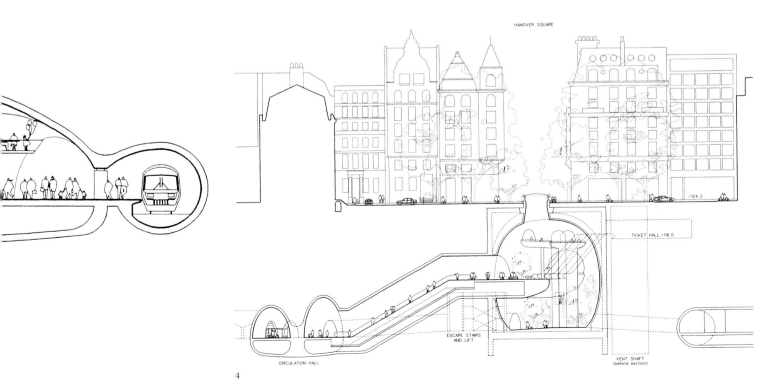

HANOVER SQUARE

TICKET HALL +116.5

+124.3

+108C

ESCAPE STAIRS
AND LIFT

VENT SHAFT
(behind section)

CIRCULATION HALL

4

Stuttgart Station

Design 1997
Stuttgart, Germany
Deutsche Bahn
71,250 square metres
Steel trusses, hollow steel members
Steel, concrete

The City of Stuttgart plans to replace its rail terminus with a new station for through-running, high-speed trains. This involves a new line running at 90 degrees to the old station and below it, crossing the city's valley heart in a tunnel. The challenge is to reinforce the historic urban form while expressing the radical design of the new station.

BDP's finalist competition entry includes a number of significant ideas. A new landscaped station piazza shifts the centre of gravity of the station more naturally to the east. The station building itself is conceived as a dramatic shaft of space covered by a light glass canopy, balancing between the old city and the new, and providing clear views of the surrounding Stuttgart hills.

Pedestrian improvements are proposed by adding mature trees and parkland into the newly created streets and public spaces as an essential part of reinforcing the continuity of the city's urban experience.

1

1   Interior of proposed station building
2   Section through new and remodelled buildings

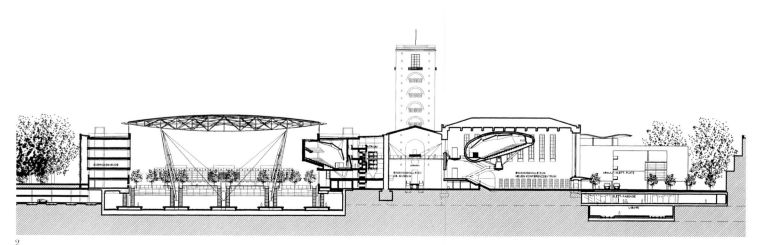

2

Rapid Transit System

Design/Completion 1995/post-2000
Bangkok, Thailand
Ital-Thai Corporation
15 kilometres, 25 stations
Segmented concrete viaduct with steel canopies
Steel and glass

The new rapid transit system in Bangkok was designed to improve substantially commuter travel facilities, as well as relieving the city's serious traffic congestion. Stations are expected to stimulate considerable redevelopment around their elevated mezzanine levels.

The railway runs on two routes, either along Bangkok's main streets or on land already owned by the Bangkok Metropolitan Administration. Due to this, and the problems of unstable ground conditions and potential flooding, it was necessary to create an elevated rail system.

BDP first produced the reference design for a contractor competition and was then novated to the winner to develop the approach successfully.

The generic station designs address all the issues, from passenger access and ticketing areas to platform canopies and operational accommodation.

Two station designs were produced, depending on passenger flow rates. The busier stations have outer tracks and central platforms, while the less busy have a central track. The station design includes a fabric canopy that admits daylight while providing weather protection and a strong station identity. All key station elements were designed as a kit of parts for integration into the engineering structure.

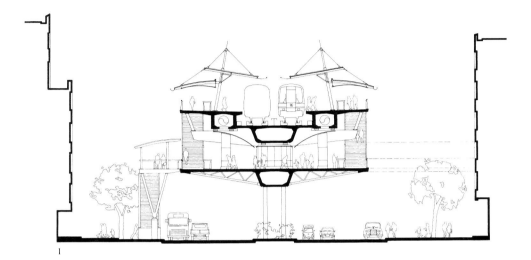

1

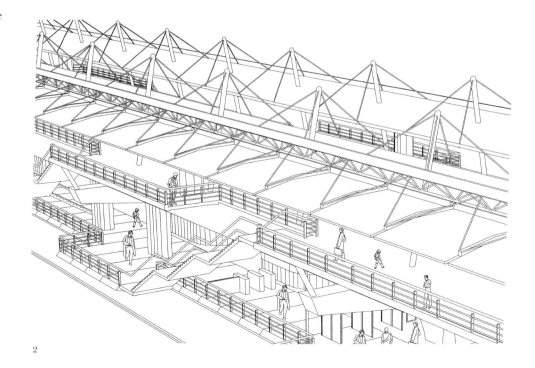

2

1   Generic station, indicationg access from buildings
    and ground level
2   Mezzanine levels of approach to platforms

New En Route Control Centre

Design/Completion 1989/1994
Swanwick, Hampshire, England
Civil Aviation Authority
42,000 square metres
In situ reinforced concrete, troughed slabs, steel roof trusses with standing triple-skinned roof, stainless steel tension cables
Cast masonry blocks, aluminium rainscreen cladding panels, planar glazing with fritted glass, aluminium windows and doors, stainless steel

The Civil Aviation Authority's New En Route Control Centre at Swanwick, Hampshire, is designed to accommodate 800 air traffic controllers and support staff. These personnel work with sophisticated systems of flight data handling and telecommunications in an environment where safety and operational integrity are paramount. When finally operational, the centre will provide a 40 per cent increase in capacity for the en route phase of flight across England and Wales, and will represent part of a major investment programme for UK air traffic services in the next century.

The project is a leading-edge, flagship development on an ecologically sensitive site. Operational spaces are surrounded by service volumes above, below and to each side, grouped to provide a low profile. The building incorporates an over-and-under configuration for the operations and telecommunications areas, flanked by plant areas and engineering distribution. This concept was developed on "loose fit" principles to facilitate up to four major refits of equipment and systems within a 40-year lifespan without causing operational disruption.

Alongside the operational facilities, the centre incorporates offices, a restaurant, a medical centre, conference and library facilities, and a multi-purpose hall. Some of these enjoy fine landscape views in contrast to the introverted operations rooms. Nature conservation was a strong theme of the total site design and includes trails and reserve areas.

1 View from across the lake
2 Aerial view
3 Reception area

1

2

3

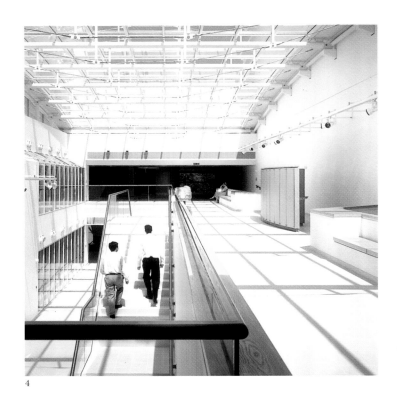

4

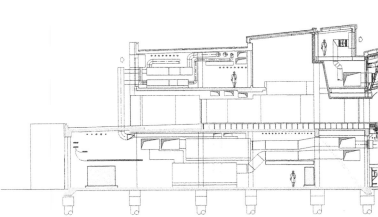

5

6

4   Internal street
5   Cross-section showing service volumes above,
    below and to each side
6   Operations room

Trading and Business

Commercial activity is the engine of our society, creating the energy and resources for all our needs. BDP is pre-eminent in the design of retail facilities across Europe. We understand traders, developers and financiers, and can add substantial value by our involvement from the earliest stage in meeting their accommodation requirements.

Workplaces in the electronic era have become the social and cultural focus of organisations, if no longer the only location for their activity. BDP's work for occupier clients and commercial developers is based on an appreciation of the new ways of working, a concern for health in the workplace, and the need for high environmental performance as well as low lifetime cost.

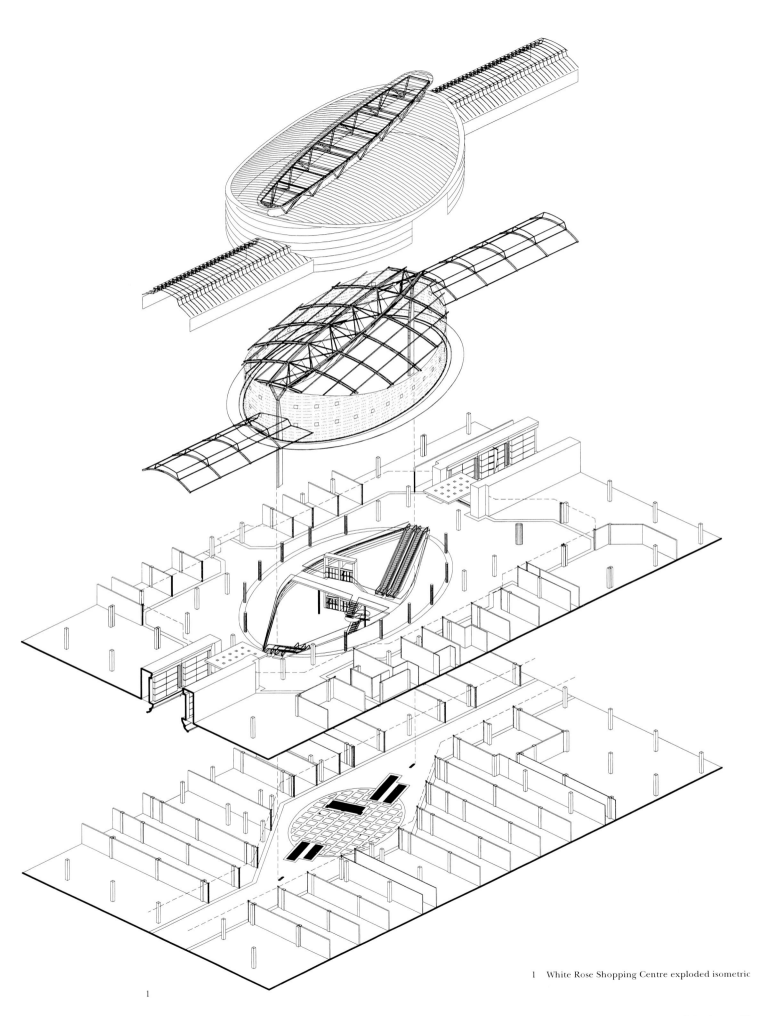

1   White Rose Shopping Centre exploded isometric

White Rose Shopping Centre

Design/Completion 1993/1997
Leeds, England
Land Securities Properties Ltd in association
with Evans of Leeds plc and Yorkshire Water
Estates
60,400 square metres
Steel frame, insitu concrete
Brickwork, metal panels, curtain wall, polished
concrete blockwork, reconstituted stone,
painted steel

This major out-of-town shopping centre comprises a mainly single-level mall with two anchor stores and a central food court at the first floor. On this steeply sloping site, great emphasis has been placed on the quality of the landscape setting.

Externally the building is designed to express its major components clearly, with large glazed canopies signalling the entrances. The mall roofs are a linking element, tying the scheme together, and the main atrium is given particularly dramatic treatment. Oval-shaped in plan, its glass roof is barrel-vaulted and provides the focus for the scheme.

The three atria and lofty malls bring high levels of natural light to the public areas, creating a bright, airy atmosphere for shoppers. Two double banks of escalators and lifts provide vertical circulation to the 650-seat food mezzanine, while a striking lighting feature provides a centrepiece to the main mall atrium. Oval forms and subtle colours distinguish this modern-style centre.

1

2

54

3

4

5

1   Extensively landscaped site
2   Main entrance
3   Double-height central atrium with food court
4   High levels of natural light
5   Smaller atrium leading to one of the anchor stores

Brent Cross, North London

Design/Completion 1993/1995 (Phase I)
1997/2001 (Phase II)
North Circular Road, London, England
Hammerson UK, Standard Life Assurance Co.
73,000 square metres (Phase I);
30,000 square metres (Phase II)
Phase I: steel frame
Phase II: concrete
Reconstituted stone, marble

Opened in 1976, Brent Cross in North London was developed as the UK's first American-style enclosed shopping centre, with air-conditioned malls and extensive free parking. The centre consists of two anchor stores and 78 units. The commission was to design improvements and extensions for the whole centre to equip it for trading into the 21st century.

Phase I involved refurbishment of all the malls and major spaces, plus the addition of 5,000 square metres of new retail space. The existing malls have been transformed by the introduction of more natural light through internal domed rooflights. Scenic lifts provide additional vertical circulation, taking pressure off the main mall and the central court.

Phase II will extend the site greatly, adding a southern mall to form a full cross. The River Brent will be realigned in a natural valley to enhance the extension. Further parking garages and a major bus station will frame a new anchor store for Marks & Spencer. The whole centre will then achieve a prominent and dynamic setting on London's major North Circular Road.

1

2

1   Natural lighting of mall extension
2   Phase II model
3   Central court dome

3

The Olympia Shopping Centre

Design/Completion 1985/1989
East Kilbride, Scotland
East Kilbride Development Corporation
17,000 square metres (retail); 9,000 square metres (leisure)
Steel frame
Brick and curtain wall, metal cladding

This retail and leisure centre was a major phase in the development of East Kilbride, a new town outside Glasgow. The East Kilbride Development Corporation aimed to transform a successful existing shopping centre into a vibrant, exciting town focus, contributing to the leisure and shopping needs of the community. The scheme includes a major public library, a multi-screen cinema, a disco and American-style diner, and the first ice rink to be incorporated into a shopping centre in the UK.

1

Centre West

Design/Completion 1997/2001
East Kilbride, Scotland
British Land, Stannifer and South Lanarkshire Council
18,600 square metres
Steel frame
Masonry base with terracotta rainscreen cladding, aluminium, glass

Centre West is a new leisure and retail development which will complement the existing Olympia Centre and increase the focus of leisure and retailing in East Kilbride.

In the three-storey building, the third floor contains the leisure facilities with a new bridge providing a connection to the existing Aquacentre. From this floor a large atrium forms the connection through two levels of shopping, arriving in a sunken winter garden.

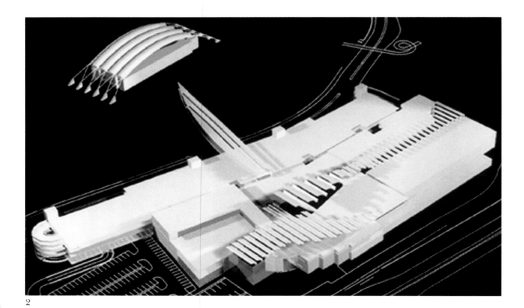

2

Braehead

Design/Completion 1997/1999
Glasgow, Scotland
Capital Shopping Centres
55,760 square metres (retail); 32,200 square metres (warehousing); 17,000 square metres (leisure)
Steel frame
Aluminium cladding panels, curtain wall

Braehead regional retail and leisure centre is the focal point of a substantial regeneration project on an 81-hectare site along the banks of the River Clyde. The shopping centre, six miles west of Glasgow city centre, will be accessible from the whole of west and central Scotland. The site masterplan also includes business space.

3

1   Ice rink, The Olympia Shopping Centre
2   Centre West model
3   Braehead site plan

Via Catarina

Design/Completion 1994/1996
Porto, Portugal
Sonae Imobiliaria
28,275 square metres
Concrete frame
Stone, glass cladding, granite floors

The Via Catarina shopping centre in the
northern Portuguese city of Porto
demonstrates how to bring life back to a
city centre by integrating a commercial
redevelopment into its historic heart.
The centre provides consumers with
modern shopping conditions without
compromising the best of the city's
old retail streetscape.

The centre is located on a site which
formerly housed the offices of the daily
newspaper *Primeiro de Janeiro*. The Neo-
Classical stone facade of the old building
is retained as the main entrance, with new
glazed facades set back on either side to
illustrate its changed role. The retail units
are designed to complement the small
scale of the existing shops in the
pedestrianised Rua de Santa Catarina,
on which the centre stands.

The design of the Via Catarina centre
exploits the steep slope of the site to
create a four-level galleria, naturally lit
under a fully glazed roof. The top level
provides a range of cafés, bars and
restaurants which overlook the galleries
inside the mall space and the streets
outside. This space provides a unique
meeting point and has become a popular
civic space for the city of Porto.

1

1   Main entrance on Rua de Santa Catarina
2   Naturally lit internal space

2

Le Grand Ciel

Design/Completion 1991/1997
Ivry-sur-Seine, Paris, France
Groupe Trema
60,000 square metres
Lightweight tubular steel, exposed steel beams
Aluminium and glass panels

The site for the Grand Ciel shopping centre was 400 metres of run-down river frontage in the suburb of Ivry near the Peripherique, Paris' urban motorway.

The design challenge was to grade the scale of the project from the grandeur of the riverside down to the finely textured urban fabric and smaller scale street scene. The contemporary design establishes a presence on the river and focuses attention on the landmark building. The dramatic "belvedere" contains three new levels of retail, with restaurants on the third floor.

The existing centre, anchored by a Carrefour hypermarket, remained open throughout the extension and refurbishment period.

1

Achrafieh Shopping Centre

Design/Completion 1998/2001
Achrafieh, Beirut, Lebanon
ABC Development
30,000 square metres (Phase I);
20,000 square metres (Phase II)
Concrete, steel
Lebanese stone and render

The project comprises a three-level retail development anchored by a department store. Due to the steep slope of the site, the third retail floor will be accessible from street level at the eastern corner. This level has been designed as an extension to the existing open street pattern, offering souk-style shopping on a more intimate scale. The internal streets will be covered to provide shade and weather protection.

A fourth floor will accommodate a restaurant, with leisure facilities laid out in a garden environment, creating a focal point for the scheme and a place of relaxation for shoppers and residents of Achrafieh.

2

3

1   Le Grand Ciel by night
2   Souk level, Achrafieh Shopping Centre
3   View to restaurant level

The Mall

Design/Completion 1994/1998
Cribbs Causeway, Bristol, England
Prudential Assurance, JT Baylis
67,360 square metres
Concrete and steel frame
Reconstituted stone, metal cladding, glass

The layout follows a contour on the sloping site; a classic dumb-bell footprint is angled twice with anchor stores of 21,400 square metres and 13,600 square metres at either end.

A 20-metre fall north–south across the site is incorporated into the design to facilitate and maximise the flow of shoppers from parking through both levels of the centre. The angles in the mall break the whole into three elements grouped around the two anchor stores and the central food court. Externally the three elements are individually expressed within an overall architectural framework.

The large area of glazed roofing floods the mall with natural light. Suspended, perforated metal solar shades diffuse the sunlight, minimising glare and excess heat. They also provide a surface with 50 per cent reflectivity against which to bounce interior light at night, greatly enhancing the character of the centre.

The wide shopping spaces feature internal planting, including 28 American palm trees. Few retail developments have such a prominent site, and the landscaping is extensive. Water features, earth sculptures, artwork and 2,500 trees combine to create a luxuriously verdant place.

1

2

1 South-facing central entrance by day
2 Avenue of trees flanking the water feature
3 Interior showing fountain and planting

3

Marks & Spencer Building

Design/Completion 1997/2001
Fenchurch Street, City of London
Marks & Spencer plc
6,975 square metres (retail); 8,361 square
metres (speculative offices)
Concrete substructure, steel frame
Portland stone, glass

This project will introduce a new building
type to the City of London—the
department store. Studies were carried out
to assess the acceptable height and
massing; these elements were of particular
concern because of the varied context,
which included both wide-scale business
streets and a small-scale conservation area.

Key features of the elevational treatment
are the horizontal expression of the
separation of office and retail floors, and a
clear identity for the office entrance on
Gracechurch Street, which integrates with
the upper office levels.

1

Henrietta House

Design/Completion 1988/1992
Henrietta Place, Westminster, London
Lynton plc, Nationale Nederlanden
14,000 square metres
Steel frame, concrete floor decks
Travertine marble, Portland stone on precast
concrete panels, granite, bronze details, Swiss
pear

This landmark building at the top of the
Bond Street vista was conceived as a
strongly contextual design in the West End
of London. Essentially symmetrical, the
building's central drum forms the corner
of a notional square surrounding St
Peter's Church Vere Street; part of the
eastern half of the building is set back
slightly to reveal the drum. The street line
is maintained by detaching the ground
floor granite architraves from the recessed
bays and using them as a colonnade for a
ramp up to the raised entrance.

1   Marks & Spencer building on the corner of
     Gracechurch and Fenchurch Streets
2   Double-height entrance hall, Henrietta House
3   Henrietta House with St Peter's Church

2

3

J P Morgan European Headquarters

Design/Completion 1986/1991
City of London
Morgan Property Development Company
68,000 square metres
Steel frame
Granite-faced aluminium-framed panels,
Portland stone, anodised aluminium windows

This discreet new headquarters building was designed as a state-of-the-art financial services centre for the US merchant bank J P Morgan. The site was that of two former City of London schools, on either side of John Carpenter Street.

The height restrictions of the St Paul's Cathedral setting and the urban grid of the Whitefriars conservation area necessitated two separate, block-filling palazzos, and meant that the sites could only be fully utilised by deep connecting basements. Facades had to be retained on part of the "island" site. The need to link the retained elements and reflect the shared heritage of the Wall Street/City of London banking tradition suggested a modern Classical design.

The main site is the banking centre, which is expressed as it is organised, with two trading floors corresponding to the *piano nobile* of the Great Hall, which was carefully conserved but subtly remodelled. The island site contains office and support space with loading, storage, restaurant and services systems extending below John Carpenter Street on three levels.

1   Listed former City of London Boys' School hall
2   Metal cornice
3   View along John Carpenter Street from Victoria Embankment

1

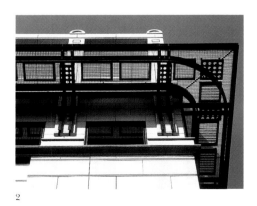

2

3

Adam Opel Haus

Design/Completion 1993/1997
Rüsselsheim, Germany
Adam Opel AG, Roland Ernst
30,000 square metres
Reinforced concrete
Sandstone and metal panels, aluminium windows and sunscreens

The new Rüsselsheim headquarters for Adam Opel AG, the General Motors car maker, is one of several new buildings which will form a campus environment created by BDP. The new headquarters building consists of two energy-efficient, mixed-mode parallel blocks each 15 metres wide, linked by a central glazed atrium that also functions as a reception space and car display area. A landscaped lake reflects the building, boosts light penetration and acts as a feature, with cars parked on square display islands.

The office accommodation is on six levels, with a cascade of escalators providing the vertical circulation. A link bridge connects staff to a Communications Centre (also designed by BDP), which houses conference and dining facilities at the heart of the campus.

The key factors in the competition-winning design are the human-scale architecture that is sympathetic to the town, and the ease of communication among those working in the building, promoted by the large floorplates and the style of circulation spaces.

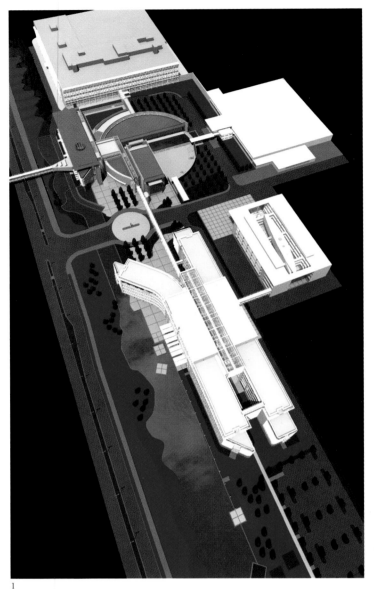

1

2

1 Aerial view of campus from the east
2 East elevation
Opposite:
   Entrance plaza with bridge leading to the
   Communications Centre

4

5

4   Cascade of escalators
5   Atrium, with reception at ground floor and café
    on first floor
6   Exterior view of atrium across landscaped
    lake, with cars on display islands

6

Halifax plc Headquarters

Design/Completion 1969/1974
Refurbishment 1993/ongoing
Halifax, Yorkshire, England
Halifax Building Society (now Halifax plc)
11,750 square metres
Steel and concrete frame
York stone, bronze anodised aluminium curtain
wall, bronze glass

In 1969 BDP was commissioned to design a new head office for the world's largest building society, the Halifax, in its modest Yorkshire home town. The bold elevated structure has become a major landmark and has won many awards (see figure 1, page 22). Twenty-five years later, the practice has returned to the building to refurbish the office floors and the catering facilities for staff and visitors.

The renovation accommodates new working practices and lifestyles but retains the geometry and character of the original design. The diagonally related structure and space modules are reinterpreted with modern lighting and frameless glazing techniques. The 5,000-square-metre main open office remains the effective core for a business that has undergone huge growth and change.

1

1   Ground floor café
2   Detail of elevated corner
3   Third floor office space

2   3

Matthew Gloag Headquarters

Design/Completion 1990/1997
Perth, Scotland
Matthew Gloag & Son Ltd
3,250 square metres
Steel frame
Sandstone, weathered zinc

Matthew Gloag & Son is a long-established Scottish company that distils and markets Famous Grouse whisky. It commissioned a new headquarters building on a greenfield site between the Kinnoull Crags and the River Tay.

The design of the building capitalises on the exceptional nature of the site; the sequence of arrival from the north screens the fine views over the river, achieving maximum impact for visitors on entering the building.

Developed as a linear, two-storey structure, the building takes full advantage of natural ventilation. The roof is formed in weathered zinc and overhangs at the south, east and west. The north elevation is traditional red sandstone, with deep window openings; the south elevation is fully glazed, recessed under the projecting canopy of the roof.

The internal organisation of the building is clearly articulated in the separation of office and support uses to either side of the entrance drum; these facilities include a restaurant with a sinuous glass wall which extends into the riverside meadow.

1

2

4

3

1   Glazed south elevation looking onto riverside meadow
2   North elevation showing entrance drum in sandstone facade
3   Building detail of company emblem
4   Staff restaurant exterior

Edinburgh Park

Design/Completion 1993/1995 (Phase I)
                          1995/1997 (Phase II)
Edinburgh, Scotland
New Edinburgh Ltd
2,787 square metres and 4,645 square metres
Steel frame structure
Stone, render, steel, anodised aluminium

The 56-hectare Edinburgh Park provides a working environment of the highest quality and forms a green extension to the city. Two office buildings by BDP provide interest and variation within a cohesive and unifying architectural theme, combining natural and traditional materials of stone and render with the modern expression of the structural steel gull wing roof.

The curved entrance porches in natural stone are punctuated with large clear planar glass openings, which at night become a major focus. Gables, which are clad in stone, are refined in detail with the introduction of balconies cantilevered beyond the face of the building, providing opportunities to enjoy views of the *lochen* (lake) and landscaped park.

1   Natural stone curved entrance porches
2   Structural gull wing roof
3   Corner gable with terrace and cantilevered balcony

Scottish Widows Headquarters

Design/Completion 1996/1998
Port Hamilton, Edinburgh, Scotland
32,600 square metres
Scottish Widows
Precast concrete
Sandstone, precast concrete, bronze-coloured
cladding

The new headquarters for the major life
assurance and pensions company, Scottish
Widows, is situated near the Edinburgh
International Conference Centre, the
Usher Hall and the ancient Edinburgh
Castle. The site is just outside the
boundary of the existing city centre
conservation area, but is still influenced by
the city's unique urban fabric, set in an
area where the geometries of the old and
new towns meet.

The new head office provides an efficient,
flexible working environment for the
company's 1,500 staff, with related
corporate, training and support functions
in linked crescent, courtyard and linear
blocks. These rise from a common double
basement of parking and support space.
The distinctive profile of the crescent
extends above the five-storey scale of its
surroundings, affording occupants superb
views of Edinburgh Castle and the city's
historic heart.

1

2

1 Aerial view
2 North elevation
3 Front entrance
4 Crescent block surrounds garden courtyard

3

4

5

6

5   Boardroom level with view of Edinburgh Castle
6   Broad stairway leading to atrium
7   Atrium at dusk
Opposite:
    View of atrium from bridge link

7

Firm Profile

Getting It Together

Few architect-led design firms can have had such a positive influence on people's lives as BDP. Working for almost 40 years across 20 countries from eight offices, BDP has designed all manner of buildings, interiors and artefacts; created new landscapes; planned new communities; and regenerated cities.

The firm's mission is to be Europe's leading building design practice, providing excellence in design and service through partnership. That partnership is between the professionals in the firm, our clients, construction firms, and the communities we serve.

BDP has three distinguishing characteristics as a design practice. The first is a philosophy of integrated working, the second is a client-centred approach to design, and the third is a formalised method of achieving continuous improvement in quality of service and product.

Integrated Working

The firm was founded in 1961 on the simple principle that buildings are best designed when all those involved work together in integrated teams under the same roof. This is in contrast to the British tradition, which has been for professions to develop separately, to educate their future members distinctly and to practice in different firms.

The BDP philosophy is increasingly relevant today, when the construction industry is being criticised by clients for its fragmentation and complexity. Pressure is growing to integrate the whole supply chain and to have the construction industry adopt the best ideas that have transformed manufacturing. But construction remains unique in that many of the technologies used in the past are still required today in repair and restoration as well as in new building. It is also highly cyclical, subject to the fortunes of national economies.

BDP's response to this challenge has been to integrate and to simplify, through partnership and process. "Partnership" refers to the sense of understanding, mutual obligation and trust that has to be established between clients, construction colleagues and the diverse elements of the firm itself.

By "process" is meant the establishment of the rules of practice, or working method, which can, when applied consistently, ensure that quality is of the highest possible standard and that effectiveness and efficiency advance continuously.

There can be difficulties in trying to remain multi-discipline, multi-location and multi-specialist, not least in achieving consistently high levels of talent and performance across all three dimensions. Nevertheless, this is what BDP endeavours to do, and with a great deal of success judged by the significance of projects won, the level of repeat commissions and the large number of design awards. Across its various locations the firm has some 15 different professions and can validly claim a high level of knowledge and experience of a similar number of sectors or building types. In 1998 BDP was voted "multi-discipline practice of the year" in a reputable UK poll.

Client-centred Approach

There is, inevitably, a tension in building design. It can arise from resolving the always unique characteristics of user needs, building location and the political context affecting them. It can occur in reconciling the desire of the architect to optimise and to distil an idea with the time and cost constraints imposed by the client. Whatever the causes, such tension can be a source of creative energy or of conflict. Where there is conflict, the frame of reference adopted by BDP for its resolution is always the needs of the client. These take priority.

Client focus can be a conservative force in relation to design imagination, but it is the force which ensures that ideas are realised and are successful. It facilitates continuity of relationships and continued improvement in design thinking and working methods. Specialist knowledge of client need in each of our sectors enables us to add value significantly and to build trust.

By responding to clients and to contexts, BDP transcends the concept of a "house style" of architecture. Our architecture is, however, rooted in the functional tradition. This tradition holds that form is derived from function and that how a thing is made should be central to how it appears. A building's "function" is fourfold:

- to provide accommodation
- to provide shelter
- to harness economic resources
- to express cultural needs.

Functionalism is therefore not prosaic, but is based on logic and performance as modified by cultural expectations. BDP's bringing together of all the relevant disciplines is justified by our belief in the relationship of form and function: engineering and economics inform architecture, a crucial example being in design for low energy use and lifetime cost-effectiveness. Client focus aligns with this philosophy: flexibility, sustainability and effectiveness all serve both clients and society.

Continuous Improvement

Throughout history, the greatest architects and engineers have sought to discover, to experience and to emulate the highest qualities in work by others. This largely intuitive process is referred to today as "benchmarking" and is becoming more systematic to avoid the variable performance in quality, time and cost criteria which is experienced by many clients of the building industry.

It is an aim of BDP to achieve quality consistently. The practice does so by several means:

- through the creation of a design focus in each location to ensure that responsibility for design leadership is in trusted hands

- through project review to identify and reinforce factors contributing to a high-quality project and to minimise known risks

- through training in working methods to ensure that our collective knowledge is applied.

On the occasion of his retirement in 1974, the advice of BDP's founder, Professor Sir George Grenfell-Baines, was to "keep going, getting better". BDP seeks continually to improve its product and process and to develop a succession of able people. The practice is at the centre of efforts to improve the performance of the whole industry, leading or participating in many official forums. At the same time it is seeking out best practice inside and outside the firm. The firm's externally audited quality system ensures compliance to best practice as it is identified and adopted.

BDP is owned by its directors and shares income and profits with its staff. The firm seeks to improve continuously the abilities of individuals and their contribution to the collective task: creating outstanding buildings that give satisfaction to clients and professionals and a proper return to BDP in which all share.

BDP is a private limited company, wholly owned by its directors. The chairman is responsible, with the board, for policy-making, and the chief executive for the day-to-day operation of the practice.

Each office and each profession in BDP has a chairman, appointed by the chief executive. Office chairmen provide the leadership in BDP locations; they have day-to-day responsibility for all aspects of their operation. Profession chairmen are responsible for the quality and training of staff in their particular professions, as well as for the appropriate resourcing of their particular professions within offices.

The finance director is responsible for the central finance, administration, risk management and IT functions serving all offices and professions, and reports to the chief executive. Corporate Communications carries out external and internal information dissemination and promotion. These firm-wide functions are mirrored at office level.

BDP also has a number of subsidiary and associated companies, established to give prominence to specialist skills or to facilitate joint-venture work in different regions of the UK and overseas.

Practice Organisation and Structure

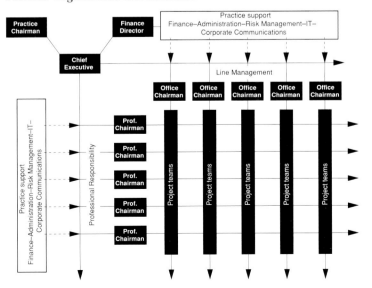

Professions

Our professions organise themselves into three broad service groups. The numbers in each discipline at June 1998 are shown in brackets.

Architectural

Architecture (233)
Interior, Product and Graphic Design (41)
Landscape Architecture (18)
Town Planning (17)

Engineering

Civil and Structural Engineering (53)
Building Services Engineering (136)
Acoustics, Lighting (8)

Management

Project Planning and Management (26)
Construction Cost Consultancy and Quantity Surveying (37)
Information Technology and Administration (178)

Specialisms

BDP has a range of practice specialisms:

Industry: especially for high-technology processes
Offices: corporate, commercial and public sector, including interiors
Retail: shopping centres and store design
Culture and Leisure: museums, performance spaces, sports facilities and tourism
Education: schools, colleges and universities, and training facilities
Health: public and private sector at all scales
Public Service: police, fire, justice and defence facilities
Urbanism: regeneration, development planning, urban and landscape design
Transport: rapid transit, rail, airports and air traffic control
Housing: for sale or rental, including student accomodation

BDP International SC

BDP has developed a network of joint ventures and associations with like-minded design practices across Europe. It is now formalised as BDP International Société Co-opérative with four major European design consultancy members: Arquitectura Langdon SA in Spain, Building Design Partnership in the UK and Ireland, Groupe 6 in France and PBR Planungsbüro Rohling AG in Germany. The grouping of more than 1,100 people provides clients with a comprehensive range of skills and a capability to work on innovative projects in the firms' home countries and beyond. Members also bring new specialisms in health-care, museums, tourism and hotel facilities.

Chronology

Pre-1960s

BDP's founder, Professor Sir George Grenfell-Baines, set up practice as an architect in Preston, Lancashire, in 1937. Four years later he teamed up with two other Preston practices and the Grenfell-Baines Group was born, later becoming Grenfell-Baines and Hargreaves. Expansion in various locations in the north continued throughout the 1940s and 1950s. Grenfell-Baines was appointed to design a building for the 1951 Festival of Britain in London. A Manchester office was set up in 1956 and a London office in 1959.

1960s

Building Design Partnership was launched as a multi-disciplinary practice in 1961. Large hospital and university projects helped to build it into a major practice, while planning work in Belfast led to the opening of a Belfast office. Grenfell-Baines led the development of the RIBA Plan of Work and became a vice president of the RIBA. BDP won its first major corporate headquarters commissions, and defence projects led to offices in Aldershot and Guildford.

1970s

At the start of the decade the firm employed some 500 staff. The retail specialism began, the practice won RIBA and Europa Nostra awards for a series of landmark projects, and a Glasgow office was established. Grenfell-Baines retired to become Professor of Architecture at the University of Sheffield and set up a Sheffield office, which was later adopted by BDP.

1980s

Rapid growth of private sector work and a decline in public sector commissions took place within the context of changes in the UK economy. In the City of London, a financial services boom fuelled a period of office expansion. The firm was 1,000 strong in 1985. Infrastructure projects, notably the Channel Tunnel terminal, widened the practice's specialisms.

1990s

A deep recession from 1990 to 1993 led to restructuring, a move towards a more European practice and the formation of BDP International SC. The firm's UK offices were consolidated in London, Manchester, Sheffield, Glasgow, and Belfast, and a new office was opened in Dublin. The private sector recovery was based on specialisms in retail, high technology industry, and cultural and leisure buildings. National lottery and public–private partnership concepts fuelled a revival in the firm's UK public building work. BDP is working in 20 countries around the world.

Selected Awards 1989–1998

1998

Multi-disciplinary Practice of the Year
Building Awards

RBA Regional Award
Catherine Cookson Reading Room
Sunderland University, Phase II
Sunderland

Civic Trust Award
Sunderland University, Phase I,
Sunderland

Civic Trust Commendation
New Number 1 Court and Broadcast Centre
All England Lawn Tennis and Croquet Club
Wimbledon, London

ICSC (Europe) Commendation
International Council of Shopping Centres
White Rose Centre
Leeds, Yorkshire

1997

BCSC Award
British Council of Shopping Centres
White Rose Centre
Leeds, Yorkshire

Building Conservation Award
Royal Institute of Chartered Surveyors
Plas Mawr
Conwy, Wales

Civic Trust Commendation
Matthew Gloag Headquarters
Perth, Scotland

ICSC (USA) Certificate of Merit
Brent Cross, Phase I
London

ICSC (Europe) Commendation
Brent Cross, Phase I
London

ICSC (Europe) Award
Via Catarina
Porto, Portugal

Best Shopping Centre Award
MIPIM (International Property Market)
Via Catarina
Porto, Portugal

1996

RIBA Regional Commendation
Grimsby Auditorium
Grimsby, Yorkshire

RIBA Regional Award
Inland Revenue
East Kilbride, Scotland

BCSC Award
Brent Cross, Phase I
London

1995

British Council for Offices Award
Inland Revenue
Durrington, West Sussex

Building of the Year Award
Royal Fine Art Commission/Sunday Times
Sunderland University, Phase I
Sunderland

RIBA Regional Award
Sunderland University, Phase I
Sunderland

Best Practice Award
British Urban Regeneration Association
Eureka! The Children's Museum
Halifax, Yorkshire

1994

RIBA Regional Award
Sheffield Hallam University Phase I & IA
North Yorkshire

Civic Trust Commendation
The Buttermarket
Ipswich, Suffolk

Europa Nostra Diploma of Merit
Christie Building
University of Manchester

Best Practice Award
British Urban Regeneration Association
Donegall Pass
Belfast, Northern Ireland

ICSC (Europe) Award
Longmarket
Canterbury, Kent

Civic Trust Commendation
Splash Leisure Pool
Dunbar, Scotland

1993

RIBA Regional Commendation
Smith & Nephew Group Research Centre
York Science Park, Yorkshire

RIBA Commendation
Eureka! The Children's Museum
Halifax, Yorkshire

RIBA Regional Award
Splash Leisure Pool
Dunbar, Scotland

BCSC Commendation
The Bentall Centre
Kingston, Surrey

High Commendation
British Construction Industry
Channel Tunnel UK Terminal
Folkestone, Kent

1992

RIBA Regional Award
St George's Library, University of Sheffield
North Yorkshire

Civic Trust Commendation
JP Morgan European Headquarters
London

MIPIM/Le Moniteur Commendation
Cannon Bridge Air Rights Development
London

Civic Trust Award (Northern Ireland)
Castle Court Shopping Centre
Belfast

Scottish Civic Trust Award
Atlantic Quay
The Broomielaw, Glasgow

BALI National Landscape Award of Merit
Cannon Bridge Roof Garden
London

1991

RIBA Regional Award
38 Carver Street
Sheffield, North Yorkshire

European Museum of the Year Commendation
Museum of Science and Industry
Manchester

ICSC (Europe) Award
The Olympia Shopping Centre
East Kilbride, Scotland

Regeneration of Scotland Commendation
Atlantic Quay
The Broomielaw, Glasgow

1990

Museum of the Year Award
Museum of Science and Industry
Manchester

RIBA Regional Award
Refuge Assurance HQ
Wilmslow, Cheshire

Civic Trust Commendation
Refuge Assurance HQ
Wilmslow, Cheshire

Europa Nostra Diploma of Merit
Whiteleys of Bayswater
London

RIBA Regional Award
Whiteleys of Bayswater
London

Royal Institute of Architects of Ireland Award
CastleCourt Shopping Centre
Belfast, Northern Ireland

BCSC Award ICSC Certificate of Merit
The Olympia Shopping Centre
East Kilbride, Scotland

1989

Office of the Year Award
Refuge Assurance HQ
Wilmslow, Cheshire

RIBA Regional Award
Museum of Science and Industry
Manchester

Bibliography

Articles on BDP projects

Barrett, John, Derek Lawson, Ken Butler, Ted Barton, Geoffrey Broadbent, Mike Jewell, Susan Dawson. "An Air of Tranquillity". (CAA, New Air Traffic Control Centre) *The Architects' Journal*, (vol. 202, no. 6, 10 August 1995), pp. 21–29.

"BDP's Grand Plans for the Royal Albert Hall." *The Architects' Journal* (vol. 203, no. 21, 30 May 1996), p. 8.

Bloomfield, Roger. "Trading Places." *The Architects' Journal* (vol. 195, no. 6, 12 February 1992), pp. 34–53. (JP Morgan European Headquarters)

Buxton, Pamela. "East–west Transfer." *Building Design* (no. 1147, 22 October 1993), pp. 1–8. (CrossRail)

Caldwell, Ian, John Bryan, Chris Croft, Rob Smith, Martin Sutcliffe, and Bryan Lawson. "The Heart of a New University." *The Architects' Journal* (vol. 199, no. 8, 23 February 1994), pp. 43–50. (Sheffield Hallam University)

Dawson, Susan. "Tunnel Vision." *AJ Focus* (vol. 7, no. 7, July 1993), pp. 13–18. (UK Channel Tunnel Terminal)

Edwards, Brian. *The Modern Station: New Approaches to Railway Architecture.* London: E&F Spon, 1997, p. 134 (Channel Tunnel UK Terminal), p. 162 (CrossRail).

"Expressing National Characteristics." *The Consulting Engineer* (no. 4, October 1995), pp. 21–23. (UK Channel Tunnel Terminal)

Fawcett, Peter. "Making Waves: BDP's Sunderland University." *Architecture Today* (no. 53, November 1994), pp. 23–28.

Gardner, Carl. "Fun Factory in Halifax." *RIBA Journal* (vol. 99, no. 9, September 1992), pp. 44–46. (Eureka! The Children's Museum)

Gorst, Thom. "Futures Market: BDP at Brent Cross." *Architecture Today* (no. 66, March 1996), pp. 22–28.

Ito, Kobun. "Sports Facilities." *SD Space Design* (Japan, vol. 32, November 1998), pp. 134–137. (New No. 1 Court and Broadcast Centre, Wimbledon)

Lewis, Penny, Simon Inglis, Colin Davies, and Richard Saxon. "Not Just Anyone for Tennis." *RIBA Journal* (August 1997), pp. 1–32. (New Number 1 Court and Broadcast Centre, Wimbledon)

McGuirk, Tony, Nicholas Derbyshire, Derek Pike, Susan Dawson. "A Unique Transport Interchange." *The Architects' Journal* (vol. 199, no. 19, 11 May 1994), pp. 41–51. (UK Channel Tunnel Terminal)

McIver, Alastair. "The Vision: Wimbledon's Grass Act Stands Alone in Battle of the Slams." *Tennis World* (November 1994), pp. 4–9.

Morrison, Jim. "On the Buses." *Perspective: The Journal of the Royal Society of Ulster Architects* (vol. 4, no. 5, May–June 1996), pp. 25–31. (Bus centre, Laganside Regeneration)

Murphy, Richard. "Landed Gently." *RIBA Journal* (vol. 103, no. 7, July 1996), pp. 36–43. (Matthew Gloag Headquarters)

Murray, Peter & Stephen Trombley. *Britain.* ADT Modern Architecture Guide series. Architecture Design and Technology Press/Van Nostrand Reinhold, 1990, p. 148. (Halifax Building Society Headquarters)

"Mutual Benefit: BDP Returns to Halifax to Update a 70s' Classic." *Architecture Today* (no. 77, April 1997), pp. 48–51.

Nuttgens, Patrick. *Understanding Modern Architecture.* London: Unwin Hyman, 1988, pp. 162–163. (Halifax Building Society Headquarters)

Pepper, Simon. "Retail Landscape: BDP's White Rose Centre." *Architecture Today* (no. 81, September 1997), pp. 42–48.

Rattray, Charles. "Capital Investment: BDP's Scottish Widows Headquarters." *Architecture Today* (no. 89, July 1998), pp. 38–46.

Singmaster, Deborah. "Back from the Brink of Collapse." *The Architects' Journal* (vol. 206, no. 18, 13 November 1997), pp. 43–45. (Plas Mawr)

Spring, Martin. "Points of Departure." *Building* (vol. 259, no. 8, 25 February 1994), pp. 36–41. (UK Channel Tunnel Terminal)

Spring, Martin. "Slick and Span." *Building* (vol. 262, no. 5, 7 February 1997), pp. 56–58. (National Maritime Museum)

Stungo, Naomi. "Bangkok Mass Rapid Transit." *RIBA Journal* (vol. 102, no. 6, June 1995), pp. 16–17.

Webb, Mark. "Court in the Act: Wimbledon's New Look." *Stadium & Arena Management* (vol. 1, no. 3, April 1997), pp. 20–22.

Wright, Anne, Tony McGuirk, Chris Harding, Farah Jahanpour, Bob Spittle, Paul Foster, Brian Edwards, Leslie Fair, and Susan Dawson. "A Gentle Learning Curve." *The Architects' Journal* (vol. 205, no. 12, 27 March 1997), pp. 25–35. (St Peter's Campus, University of Sunderland, Phase II)

Wright, Lance. "Building Society Headquarters, Halifax, Yorkshire." *The Architectural Review* (no. 157, April 1975), pp. 233–244.

Articles on BDP

Adamson, Niki. "A Double Celebration for BDP: Silver and Gold." *Retail* (vol. 4, no. 3, winter 1986), pp. 17–18.

Davies, Colin. "BDP 1: Building on the Professions." *The Architects' Journal* (vol. 184, no. 46, 12 November 1986), pp. 87–90.

Davies, Colin. "BDP 2: A Matter of Discipline." *The Architects' Journal* (vol. 184, no. 47, 19 November 1986), pp. 79–82.

Davies, Colin. "BDP 3: Setting Standards." *The Architects' Journal* (vol. 184, no. 48, 26 November 1986), pp. 73–75.

Davies, Colin. "BDP 4: Running the Shop." *The Architects' Journal* (vol. 184, no. 49, 3 December 1986), pp. 61–62.

Davies, Colin. "Responsibility, Recognition and Reward." *World Architecture* (no. 29, 1994), pp. 88–95.

Delaney, Katrina. "Multi-discipline Put into Practice." *Estates Times* (vol. 872, 28 November 1986), p. 35.

Finch, Paul. "Silver & Gold." *Building Design* (no. 816, 12 December 1986), pp. 12–15.

Hill, Ed. "A Jubilant Partnership." *Building* (vol. 251, no. 44, 7 November 1986), pp. 30–33.

Moore, Mark. "Bringing it In-house." *Chartered Quantity Surveyor* (vol. 9, no. 5, December 1986), pp. 25–29.

Pearman, Hugh. *Contemporary World Architecture.* London: Phaidon Press Ltd, 1998, pp. 131 (St Peter's Campus, University of Sunderland), 401 (New No. 1 Court, Wimbledon), 481 (BDP).